HOME IS WHERE MY PEOPLE ARE

The Roads That Lead Us to Where We Belong

Sophie Hudson

Tyndale House Publishers, Inc.
Carol Stream, Illinois

Visit Tyndale online at www.tyndale.com.

TYNDALE and Tyndale's quill logo are registered trademarks of Tyndale House Publishers, Inc.

Home Is Where My People Are: The Roads That Lead Us to Where We Belong

Designed by Jacqueline L. Nuñez

Edited by Stephanie Rische

Published in association with William K. Jensen Literary Agency, 119 Bampton Court, Eugene, Oregon 97404.

Library of Congress Cataloging-in-Publication Data

Hudson, Sophie.
   Home is where my people are : the roads that lead us to where we belong / Sophie Hudson.
      pages cm
   ISBN 978-1-4143-9173-1 (sc)
1. Hudson, Sophie. 2. Christian biography—Southern States. 3. Christian life. I. Title.
   BR1725.H7255A3 2015
   277.3'083092—dc23
   [B]   2014040745

Printed in the United States of America

21	20	19	18	17	16	15
7	6	5	4	3	2	1

For Sister, who is more loyal to her people than anyone I know,
and who makes wherever we are feel like home. xoxo

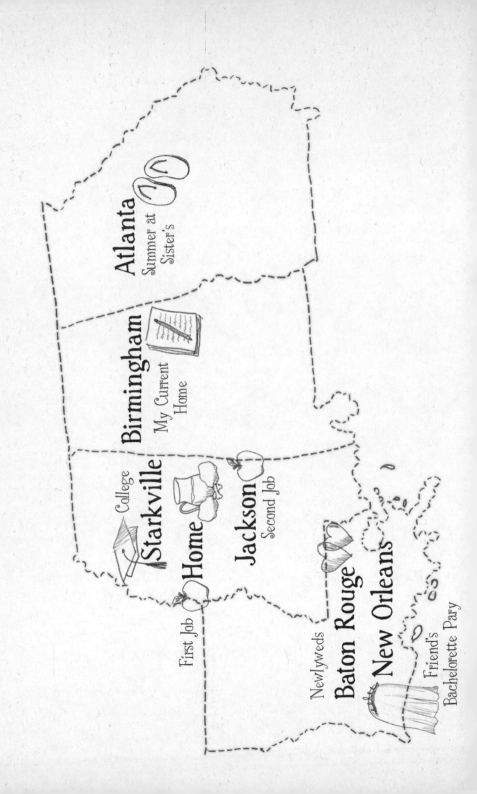

Atlanta
Summer at Sister's

Birmingham
My Current Home

Starkville
College

Home
First Job

Jackson
Second Job

Baton Rouge
Newlyweds

New Orleans
Friend's
Bachelorette Party

CONTENTS

A QUICK NOTE ABOUT SOME THINGS

THE THING ABOUT writing books is that sometimes it makes me wish I were a robot.

I mean, not physically, really. Because robots move sort of awkwardly and seem to need a good bit of oil and are pretty much stuck between a rock and a hard place if they're at a wedding and the band plays "Hard to Handle" by the Black Crowes.

Because you know what's tough for robots? Jumping on the dance floor and BREAKING IT DOWN.

But robots, as best I understand from frequent viewings of *The Jetsons* and also *Star Wars*, have incredible memories. This probably has something to do with the fact that they're computers, though I'm not exactly sure since I'm not very science-y. But when I was writing this book that you're holding—a book that covers a big ole chunk of my life—I really wished that I had more robot- or computer-like qualities. I did my best to get the facts as accurate as I could, but since I am not in fact a robot, I was dependent on my very human memory. I'm well aware that my memories may differ from other people's, but I did the very best I could.

Also, I changed a few names and details when I was trying to protect people from the Google, and occasionally I rearranged the order of certain events so that the timeline wouldn't make your head explode.

I feel like that's a good goal for an author: *try not to make your readers' heads explode*.

No need to thank me for that, by the way. It's just a free service that I like to provide.

Aside from a few minor changes and adjustments, though, these are real stories about the real lives of real people. Keep in mind that I have no doubt exaggerated some of the details since I'm Southern and we seem to have an unspoken adage in this part of the country: *If the story doesn't get a little bit bigger every time you tell it, you're telling it wrong.*

Unfortunately, there are no stories about robots. I do hope that's not a deal breaker.

Thanks for reading, y'all.

THAT TIME I WAS GOING TO A PARADE

I'VE ALWAYS HAD a thing about home.

And I'm certainly not the only one. I mean, have you taken a look around the Internet lately? There are thousands of websites dedicated to building homes and furnishing homes and keeping homes and doing all the other home-related activities. America may be a nation that can't figure out how to balance its own budget, but by diggity we are a people that can create and also implement incredibly detailed instructions in order to transform pumpkins into festive decorative items.

Don't even get me started about what people are doing with gourds these days. Suffice it to say that the gourds are enjoying a bit of a home-decor renaissance.

But my lifelong affection for home has nothing to do with pumpkins or gourds or even the lesser-utilized squash. However, it *can* be traced back to a state that you spell with four *s*'s, four *i*'s, and a couple of *p*'s thrown in for good measure.

(I'm talking about Mississippi.)

(I felt like I needed to go ahead and write it out in case you've been singing the fifty states song in your head and trying to figure out which state I'm talking about.)

(Sometimes the most obvious answers are the toughest.)

Mississippi is where I was born and raised. My beloved mother-in-law, Martha, might take issue with my choice of words in that last sentence, and she'd probably remind me, "You raise cattle and crops! But you rear children! So you were reared! You weren't raised!" But whether I was raised or reared or some combination of the two, I grew up in Myrtlewood, Mississippi, where I spent the first seventeen years of my life in the same red brick house with the same two parents. Considering how common it's become over the last few decades for people to move around and change spouses and blend families, I believe the level of stability I enjoyed is what sociologists would call *a cultural anomaly*. Back then, though, it was nothing unusual, and while life wasn't perfect, it was simple. And steady. And sweet.

Once I went off to college, though, I made up for lost time as far as moving was concerned. I must have moved eight times over the next ten years, but besides one summer in Georgia, I always lived somewhere inside the geographical comfort zone of the Magnolia State. I was happy to be hemmed in on all sides by the Mississippi River, the Gulf of Mexico, and the states of Louisiana, Alabama, and Tennessee. I didn't see any reason why I would ever leave.

But then, when I was twenty-seven, I married a boy who was living in Louisiana. Since living in the same place is generally a solid choice when you've promised to spend the rest of your life with someone, I packed up all my stuff and moved my newlywed self to Baton Rouge. Truth be told, I was kind of excited to start married life in a new place. But after a few weeks, reality started to set in, and make no mistake: even though I enjoyed and appreciated all the things that make south Louisiana unique and charming and pretty much like nowhere else on earth, I missed Mississippi with everything in me.

I continued to miss Mississippi for the next three years.

Eventually David and I realized that it was the right time for us to make our first big move as a couple, so we left bayou country and moved to Birmingham, Alabama. That's another story in and of itself, and I'm gonna tell it in just a little bit. Or at least I'll tell the important parts of it. If I told you the whole thing, you'd probably lapse into a twitching fit and your eyes would roll way back in your head. And while I don't mean to mind your business, you should really demand more than that from your books. At least in my opinion.

Anyway. We moved to Birmingham. We settled in. We went to work. We bought a house. We joined a church. We felt comfortable here.

But it was hard for me to shake the feeling that home—my *real* home— was one state to the west, where the drawl is just the tiniest bit more pronounced and magnolia trees line the interstates, swaying like sweet old ladies who open their screen doors and beckon you to come on in.

• • •

Now. If you're thinking that this is a book where I'm going to tell you how to do some things—like how to turn a cross-country move into an adventure for your family or how to follow my simple eighty-nine-step plan for creating a more welcoming living environment—let me put your mind at ease. I don't have any advice. Or strategies. Or plans.

But what I do have are some stories.

Because what I've come to know way down deep in my heart is this: whether we've lived in the same house for forty-two years or we find ourselves moving every fourteen months, God has a purpose in every place. I don't want to overstate it, of course, but it's good to remember a little something called the Old Testament. And if I could play Captain Obvious for just one second, let me please point out that those Israelites—THEY MOVED AROUND A LOT.

And you know what? Not one bit of that moving around caught God by surprise. He ordained every single step of their journey. Take out any one stop on the long desert road, and you pretty much alter the whole course of human history.

Look at Jesus, for instance (yes, I just threw down the Jesus gauntlet on page xv of the book; clearly I am NOT MESSING AROUND). In order for His birth and death and resurrection to happen, God had to orchestrate some significant historical events to get that family line from point A to point B, you know? It took a mighty long time to move those puzzle pieces from Eden to Jerusalem.

So where we were, where we are, where we're going—*it matters.* And even if you think that God can't possibly have a plan for you and where you live doesn't matter to Him and if He was so concerned about your location, then HE WOULD HAVE MADE SURE THERE WAS A TARGET CLOSER TO YOUR HOUSE, then just hold on for a little while. Stay with me.

Please and thank you.

(See? Those Mississippi roots run deep.)

• • •

Birmingham, as it turned out, was a really good move for us. Next year will be our fifteenth year here, and if we hold to fifteenth-anniversary traditions, I guess that means that David and I need to buy Birmingham a piece of crystal or something. I'm sure a cut crystal vase would make a lovely adornment on the end of Vulcan's spear.

But truth be told, we owe Birmingham a lot more than a gift from the "For the Home" department at the Belks. This place has been mighty good to us. It's been mighty good *for* us.

And about two years ago, something happened that made me reframe my perception of the whole "home" thing.

(And just to be clear: I now love Birmingham with an enthusiasm that might make you a little bit uncomfortable if we were talking in person.)

(Seriously. It's kind of ridiculous. I have been known to get visibly emotional when I talk about it.)

(Because that's totally normal.)

So a few years ago, I picked up our little boy, Alex, in the carpool line and headed to a nearby café so we could grab a quick snack before his school's homecoming parade began. He was in second grade at the time, and we had just turned out of the parking lot onto a fairly busy road when I spotted an SUV that I recognized heading toward us in the other lane. I grinned and waved, and the other driver honked his horn while three or four teenagers leaned out the windows and screamed, "HEYYYYY, MRS. HUDSON!" as they drove by.

On the surface it was just a typical Friday afternoon in a beautiful Southern city. No big deal, right?

But for whatever reason, in that moment I was vividly aware of a profound feeling of familiarity—a confidence in being known by the people who belong to a place. I don't know that I'd ever felt that so strongly as an adult. And as I pondered the unexpected sweetness of the moment, I was surprised to realize that I was wiping tears from my eyes.

It was such an ordinary thing—essentially I'd just waved at some people I knew and then continued to drive down the road. Somehow, though, it felt like an epiphany. Because what I realized on that sunny fall afternoon was that Birmingham is so much more than just a place where we live.

It really is *home*.

So is Mississippi, of course. It doesn't have to be an either-or proposition. It took me a long time to figure that out.

And for the rest of the day, there was one specific thought that ran on a loop in my brain.

Home is where my people are.

• • •

It's easy, I think, to go through life believing we can satisfy our longing for home with a three-bedroom, two-bath slice of the American dream that we mortgage at 4 percent interest and pay for over the course of thirty years. But it seems to me that, in our deepest places, what we're really looking for is to belong, to be seen, and to be known. And what we sometimes miss in all our searching for the perfect spot to set up camp, so to speak, is that wherever we are—whether it's short term or long term—we can count on the fact that God is at work in the journey.

So here's what I know way down deep in my bones: at every stop in the road—no matter what the physical address happens to be—the Lord shows Himself to be so gracious. So loving. So intentional. So consistent. So kind. Even when our circumstances aren't easy.

Certainly that's been the case in my life. I have a feeling that it's been true in yours, too.

•   •   •

I'm pretty sure that Holden Gully and his buddies had no idea what kind of reaction they sparked that day when they honked the horn and waved at me on Altadena Road. They were just a bunch of seventeen-year-olds who saw a familiar face on the way to the homecoming parade.

But that moment, for whatever reason, has stayed with me. It was a vivid, visceral reminder that God doesn't just give us a place (though certainly in David's and my case, Birmingham would be more than enough since it is, in fact, the best of all the cities)—He gives us people.

Family. Childhood friends. College friends. The older couple who lived next door when you'd been married all of eight months and weren't entirely sure you'd make it to nine. The seemingly random person down the street who turned out to be connected to your life in more ways than you can count. We could list example after example after example.

And those places and those people? They teach us, shape us, refine us.

Those places and people change everything, y'all.

And to really and truly understand that, to see how intricately God has woven together all the threads and pieces and parts of our lives—well, sometimes we just have to look at things a little closer.

We might be surprised by what we see.

CHAPTER 1

SURPRISINGLY, THE FRIED CHICKEN IS NOT MY DOMINANT MEMORY

I'M JUST GONNA jump straight into the deep end and tell you something that I believe with everything in me.

I hope it's not controversial. But I need to say it.

Ready?

Google Maps is a wonder, y'all.

Seriously.

Because for the last ten minutes, I've been wandering up and down the road where I grew up in Myrtlewood, Mississippi. I happen to be sitting in a room off of my kitchen right here in Birmingham, Alabama, mind you, but thanks to my computer and the interwebs and some Wi-Fi hot spot web-based video technology (clearly I am well versed in technical language), I've been standing in front of Mama and Daddy's old house. Looking around. Taking it in. Wondering what happened to all the pine trees that towered over the backyard and provided some shade when I would perform my elaborate gymnastics routines.

(Please know that when I say *elaborate*, what I really mean is "two front somersaults and a cartwheel.")

For the most part, the house looks like it always has. There's still a front porch that wasn't quite as deep as what Mama had wanted when they built the house back in the early sixties, and I can't help but smile when I see the three newel posts that weren't as substantial as Mama would have liked.

That porch was an ongoing source of frustration—at least twice a year Mama wanted to rip the roof off of it and start over. I think she had visions of a sweeping Southern facade: something that would be *Southern Living* cover-worthy, something that would easily accommodate four or five full-size rocking chairs. However, Mama and Daddy's construction budget dictated otherwise. And as a child of the Depression, Mama learned early on that there was always a way to do a lot with a little, so she made the best of it. She'd line that porch with her gorgeous asparagus ferns, add a few throw pillows to the deacon's bench, and make sure there was something pretty blooming right by the front door.

It's a Southern woman's unspoken motto, really: When life gives you imperfect porch proportions, *accessorize, accessorize, accessorize.*

• • •

It was 1963 when my parents found the land where they'd eventually build their house. I don't remember one thing about that time because, well, I wasn't alive, but Sister has filled me in on most of the details. Mama and Daddy paid cash for twelve acres on a dirt road (I know it sounds like I'm writing a country song, but bear with me), and after Daddy decided that he'd work as his own contractor to save on construction costs, they drew up plans for their own little parcel of paradise.

According to Sister, building the house was all manner of lively. Daddy salvaged some bricks from an old house across the road—he and Mama wanted to use them for the fireplace—but unfortunately the gentleman who actually built the fireplace liked to have a beer or nine as he worked. The chimney, which was on the back of the house, ended up being too short, a fact that annoyed Mama to no end since she'd wanted the chimney to be visible from the front yard. There was also an issue with the chimney's craftsmanship: it never drew smoke correctly, so smoke would back up into the den on occasion, and really, what good is a fire in the fireplace if you have to open all the windows to ensure proper ventilation?

Granted, Mama wanted her guests to be warm, but she certainly didn't want them to suffer from smoke inhalation.

In some ways, though, the house was ahead of its time. It was one of the first all-electric houses in the area, and Mama's kitchen featured Coppertone-brown appliances that were all the rage in the sixties and seventies. Since Mama has always loved to decorate, she took charge of the finishes and trims, too. She bedecked the master bath with turquoise and light blue tile and selected a more minimalist black and white tile in the kids' bath. She elected to use a good-quality wood for her closets, baseboards, windows, and door frames, so there wasn't an inch of painted wood anywhere in the house. Once the house was finished and all of her furniture was in place, she'd managed to achieve a bit of Danish flair right there in the piney woods of central Mississippi.

Exactly where you'd expect to find it, right?

• • •

By the time I was old enough to have any awareness at all about where I lived, Mama, Daddy, Sister, and Brother had been in the "new" house for almost a decade. They'd shifted and adjusted to make room for me, so Sister and I shared the master bedroom for a few years while Mama and Daddy took up residence in a smaller bedroom at the front of the house. I thought all five-year-olds got to have a bathroom adjacent to their rooms, and it wasn't until I was much older that I realized how Mama and Daddy had sacrificed their space for us.

Life in the house that my parents built wasn't perfect by any stretch of the imagination. There were tensions and arguments and resentments. Sister and I both would tell you that we cried more tears in that house than we have in any place since (teenage drama is hard, y'all). And—just in case you've forgotten—please let me remind you that MAMA WAS UNHAPPY WITH THE PROPORTIONS OF THE FRONT PORCH.

Real problems. We had 'em.

But we also had something else: stability. Daddy faithfully went to work every morning, and even though he never said a word about it, we all knew that he excelled at his job. Mama stayed home and worked just as hard in our house. The two of them shuttled kids to piano lessons and ball games and dance lessons and cheerleading practices and 4-H meetings. They put three kids through college, paid off their house, and tirelessly served their church and their community.

I don't recall a single time when they lectured us about responsibility. But they didn't have to.

Their actions preached that sermon just fine.

• • •

When I type in Mama and Daddy's old address on "the Google," as Mama calls it, the street view puts me smack-dab in the middle of an intersection about a mile from the house itself. I've traveled through that intersection thousands of times—to the point that I have all of its options memorized.

If I go east, I'll pass the Pak-A-Sak (site of many an orange slushie when I was a little girl), the swim club where I spent countless summer days (in this case, "swim club" is really just another way of saying "affordable swimming pool option located on the edge of someone's woods"), and the big Victorian house that belonged to the Yarbroughs and then the Hollands. Sister and Barry's wedding reception was there, as was my bridal luncheon. And if I keep moving past the Hollands' old house, I'll eventually pass the street where my friend Amanda lived, the turn that leads to my elementary school, and the Baptist church where our next-door neighbors were members. I went to VBS at that church from first through sixth grade. That's why I can't look at the steeple without thinking of Bible drills and strawberry Kool-Aid.

If I go north, I'll see every house and landmark I passed on the way to Aunt Choxie and Uncle Joe's or to my high school or to the Winn-Dixie where Mama often sent me to buy some grocery item she'd forgotten. Since that way led to most of my friends' houses, it was the road I traveled more than any other once I started driving. There's not an unfamiliar turn or curve; even now I'm almost certain that you could spin me around ten times, put me in the driver's seat, and I'd be able to drive it blindfolded. That road led to Methodist Youth Fellowship on Sunday nights when I was in high school, and a few years later, I followed it all the way out to Highway 45, where I turned left and drove to Starkville for college. In so many ways it was the path to independence. The fact that it ran straight by my favorite fried chicken place didn't hurt one bit either.

(Sometimes I would visit the drive-thru for a little of that fried chicken before I'd start the journey back to Starkville.)

(It was my little pre-travel secret.)

(Except for the fact that if you'd scrutinized my freshman year weight gain, you would have eventually said, "I believe she's consuming more than her fair share of fried chicken.")

If I click south at that intersection, I'll dead-end at the building where my friend Kimberly and I used to take aerobics classes back when people wore leotards and leg warmers. Turn left, and I'll eventually end up at my friend Ricky's old house, which was where we did a whole lot of laughing and *SNL* watching in high school. Ricky's house was on the way to one of Myrtlewood's main thoroughfares, which just so happened to be the place where teenagers used to cruise up to the Sonic and back down to McDonald's on Friday and Saturday nights. I hated everything about that particular teenage ritual—mainly because the whole exercise seemed point-less to me: a waste of gas and a waste of time. Mamaw here would have rather stayed home and watched *Fantasy Island* reruns.

Head west, and well, that's the road that used to take me home. I'll pass the country store where I'd buy a copy of Jackson's *Clarion-Ledger* in the mornings so I could read whatever Rick Cleveland and Orley Hood had written about life and sports in Mississippi. I'll see the subdivision where the Haleys and the Cades used to live; we carpooled to dance lessons for a year or two, and Mrs. Haley, who had a wonderful, deep, almost-baritone voice, wore so much gardenia perfume that I developed a lifelong aversion to it.

If I continue to click my way down Pine Tree Road, I'll start to see the houses that are etched in my memory not so much for their architecture but because of the families who lived inside them: the Snowdens, the Hursts, the Gwaltneys, the Lloyds, the Saxons, the Walkers, the Bonds. I don't remember a time when I didn't know their names, when I didn't overhear Mama and Daddy talking about this person's mother passing away or that person's sister finding a new job or somebody else's son getting a scholarship to college.

That road spans the gap of most of the joys and heartaches of my childhood; it's a road that was paved with casseroles and pies and progressive dinners, a road with an extensive collection of CorningWare and Pyrex—all carefully labeled with masking tape, a name, and a five-digit telephone number. It's a road where most of the houses had a vegetable garden in the back, where neighbors swapped recipes for squash pickles and bread-and-butter pickles and pickled okra. It's a road where I shelled peas and dodged traffic on my bike and carried on long conversations about everything and nothing over the fence that separated our house from the Easoms'.

It's just a road. But it's so much more. Because it was home.

• • •

I haven't lived in that red brick house in more than twenty-five years; it has probably been five years since I've even driven past it. So I guess I expected that clicking my way down Pine Tree Road on Google Maps—and clicking to see the house where I grew up—would fill me with all sorts of nostalgia. I thought that it would prompt me to think back on all the funny and hard and awkward moments that I associate with my childhood home. I imagined I'd get to the point where the house was front and center on my computer screen, and I'd reflect long and hard about The Mistakes I Made, The Drama I Created, The Times I Cried, The Lessons I Learned.

I thought that, given our history, the house and I would have ourselves a moment. Courtesy of Google and Apple and the worldwide interweb.

But the house and I didn't really have a moment at all. Oh, the house was special—no doubt. It was special because it was ours. It was special because I grew up there. I can see so many lessons just from the way Mama and Daddy took care of those twelve acres; over the course of our time there, they remodeled, they added on, they reroofed, they painted. They raked, they mowed, they tended, they watered, they pruned, and they weeded. They figured out what was broken. They fixed it.

And Lord knows that they planted and they sowed.

But the Google Maps, as it turned out, taught me something that I wasn't really expecting.

The house is significant, yes. But really, it's only part of the story.

Because what flat-out captivates me is the road.

CHAPTER 2

THAT APOSTLES' CREED WILL TEAR YOU UP IF YOU PAY ATTENTION TO IT

I DID NOT grow up in a house where church was an option.

And I hope that doesn't sound like I'm mad about it. I'm not mad about it at all. In fact, I'm grateful. Now that I'm grown, I can recognize that *something* is going to be the center—the core—for every family, and in ours, it was church. Life at Mission Hill United Methodist was woven into and through every single part of our lives. Church was the priority—a higher one than family, I think—and it was nonnegotiable.

I've been thinking about the whole church thing a lot lately because of a discussion I had recently with a friend. She feels like once kids are a certain age—fourteen or fifteen, maybe—they should be able to decide if they want to go to church or not. I totally see where she's coming from; in fact, it took me about ten years to work through all my church-related issues once I became an adult, and I spent about six of those years trying to stay as far away from a sanctuary as I could.

But now that I'm a parent, I'm a little more old school than I ever thought I'd be. I tend to land on the same side of the fence my parents did—a side that might best be articulated this way:

If thou livest in this house,
And eateth this food,
And enjoyeth the water, power, clothing, and shelter
That thy parents hath provided—
Then thou will gettest thy tail out of bed on Sunday mornings,
And thou will goest to the church house,
Where thou will learn about the Lord in the presence of His people,
Regardless of however thou might feeleth.
Amen.

I'm not sure that you'll find that particular call to worship in *The Book of Common Prayer*.

But I'm thinking of having it engraved on our son's door frame nonetheless.

And, oh heavens—it's certainly not like I had some idyllic experience with church life when I was growing up. My parents, who were a solid 9.5 out of 10 on the Involved at Church scale, let me see all sides of it.

The good, the bad, the joyous—and sometimes even the ugly.

• • •

The fact that my daddy grew up Baptist was a source of endless curiosity to me when I was young. Mama is a fifth-generation Methodist who prayed with her whole heart that Daddy wouldn't expect her to join the Baptist church after they married, and apparently the Lord was on her side, because Daddy became a Methodist. By the time I was born, he'd been steeped in the Wesleyan tradition for almost fifteen years. He even sang in the choir at the little Methodist church where we were members, and it was hard for me to imagine him in an environment where the Apostles' Creed wasn't part and parcel of a Sunday morning service.

I was in second grade when Mama and Daddy decided to move their membership to Mission Hill UMC. Aunt Chox and Uncle Joe had been members there since they married, and while I never really quizzed Mama and Daddy about what prompted the move, I think they just felt like it would be a better fit for our family. Mission Hill was full of couples their age, and I am here to tell you that they welcomed us with open arms. Within weeks it felt like the only church I'd ever known.

Granted, I was all of seven years old. But Chox was my Sunday school teacher in the first- and second- grade class, my cousin Paige and I got to sit in church together, and all the other kids were really nice—including a boy named David Hudson who didn't go to my school but made me laugh a lot. Plus, his mama, who I called "Miss Martha," was really sweet and always gave me compliments when I was wearing a new dress.

I couldn't put my finger on it, but there was just something about that place that felt like home.

• • •

By third grade, I knew every nook and cranny of Mission Hill UMC. Mama taught an interdenominational women's exercise class at the church three mornings a week, and if I didn't feel like stretching and twisting with the leotard-wearing ladies, I'd explore the Sunday school building. I'd sneak into the room where the Friendship Class met and "teach" a quick grammar lesson on the chalkboard. Afterward I'd walk down to the nursery and wave at the babies, who were there for Mother's Day Out. I'd cross the hall to peek in the room where the ladies in macramé class were making plant holders, and then I'd amble down to the fellowship hall to practice my scales on the piano. If I happened to have a quarter in my pocket, I'd buy myself what had to be Mississippi's coldest bottle of Coke from the old drink machine next to the youth room. The youth room was where the older kids would play four square and Ping-Pong at Methodist Youth Fellowship, and sometimes I'd sit on the sofa in there and look through the latest copy of the *Upper Room* or stare at the cover of *The Way* Bible.

(*The Way* Bible was groovy, man.)

(I think that it would have been fast friends with *The Message* if it had been around at the same time.)

Eventually I'd walk up the stairs at the back of the youth room, maybe peek in the pastor's study to see what he was up to, and then I'd check in on Mrs. Nell, our faithful secretary, who surely had to have set speed records when she typed on her IBM Selectric. Sometimes I'd help Mrs. Nell fold the bulletins for the upcoming Sunday service, and I'd usually walk over to the choir room, where I'd play my scales on the piano again and look at the chalkboard to see what music the choir was rehearsing that week.

Finally, to cap off my tour, I'd go into the sanctuary, where I'd (1) pretend I was a bride walking down the aisle, (2) pretend I was a preacher delivering a message, or (3) pretend I was playing the organ.

(Sometimes I'd even turn on the organ and play a few notes.)

(I can only imagine how my improvisational melodies inspired the pastor as he prepared his sermon for the week.)

The bottom line is that I was utterly comfortable there. Perfectly at peace. Nothing was off limits. Nobody was unkind.

I was safe. In heart, body, mind, soul.

That's how church should be, don't you think?

• • •

By the time I was in fourth grade, our Sunday school crew was pretty firmly established. There were eight or nine of us who were regulars, and even if we didn't see each other during the week at school, we'd catch up in a hurry on Sunday mornings. My friend Beverly was the person I'd look forward to seeing most, and that was because she was hilarious. Her running commentary on everything we did—whether we were memorizing the books of the Bible or coloring pictures of the Good Samaritan—kept the kids and the teachers in stitches.

One year our favorite teacher, Miss Diane (well, honestly, we just called her "Diane," though in retrospect that seems very un-Southern of us and maybe even a little rude), suggested that we take up a special Lenten offering and then use that money to help a child connected to an overseas outreach program run by the Methodist church. I can't remember exactly how much we needed to sponsor a child for a year, but I'll never forget when Diane showed us a piece of paper with pictures of all the kids who needed sponsors. Beverly looked at those pictures for approximately six seconds before she said five words that David and I still repeat to this day:

"OH MY WORD, THE BONNET!"

We all sat still as stones, not having any idea what she was talking about. Then Beverly started pointing.

"Look at this little girl with the bonnet! We have to pick her! DO YOU SEE THIS BONNET?"

Beverly was adamant; there was no room for negotiating. So we picked the little girl with the bonnet, and that was that.

That was also my first experience with anything related to missions.

Please don't judge me.

• • •

Every week after Sunday school we'd have refreshments in the fellowship hall. There was always coffee, and depending on whose week it was to serve, there might be an assortment of store-bought shortbread cookies—the ones that come about two hundred to a pack. If Mama and Daddy's Sunday school class was finished with their lesson, I could usually convince Daddy to give me twenty-five cents for the Coke machine.

Mama and Daddy's class was in a tiny room at the end of the fellowship hall, and the members were so faithful that I can still name many of them today: Mama and Daddy, Martha, Chox and Joe, the Partridges, the Beavers, the Turnages, the Kents, the Dixons, the Williamsons, the Walkers, and the Torrances. Mr. Torrance liked to place his folding chair right outside the doorway so that he could hear the lesson but not see who was teaching it, and he'd chew on a cigar from the opening prayer to the closing prayer since he couldn't smoke in church. He actually became my signal in terms of knowing if the class was finished or not: Mr. Torrance still sitting in the doorway chewing on his cigar = class was in session; Mr. Torrance standing outside the doorway and chewing on his cigar = class was over. It was a method as reliable as a ringing school bell.

After I'd (hopefully) grabbed some cookies and a Coke, I'd visit for a few minutes with Mama and Daddy's friends, then find Chox so we could walk up to "big church." Since Mama and Daddy both sang in the choir,

I sat with Chox and Joe every single Sunday—unless I was an acolyte, in which case I had to sit in the front row. If we walked into the sanctuary the back way, we'd always stop to speak to my friend Beverly's parents and the Williamsons on the way to our normal row. If we came in from the outside entrance, we'd get a bulletin from Mr. Fountain, who always made sure to count attendance and adjust the thermostat according to the weather.

Usually the service would pass without incident. Mrs. Bernice Nicholson would play the call to worship on the piano, and the choir would enter the sanctuary. We'd stand and sing the first hymn together, and then afterward we'd have a responsive reading. I'd read every word aloud because I knew my parents were watching from the choir loft even when they looked like they weren't, but normally it all sounded sort of poetic and distant to me. The pastor would read the words in regular type, and we'd respond with the words in bold.

It is good to give thanks to the Lord,
    to sing praises to your name, O Most High;
to declare your steadfast love in the morning,
    and your faithfulness by night,
to the music of the lute and the harp,
    to the melody of the lyre,
For you, O Lord, have made me glad by your work;
    at the works of your hands I sing for joy.
#811, UNITED METHODIST HYMNAL

After that we'd say the Apostles' Creed. I'd memorized the whole thing by the time I was three, but I'll be the first to admit that it took a good while longer for the meaning of those words to settle in. Sometimes my heart needs time to catch up to my head.

We'd sing another hymn, and if there was anyone with an even remotely operatic voice singing the offertory (or a solo during the anthem, for that matter), Chox would move between Paige and me. There was no worse church-service scenario than an operatic singer, simply because Paige and I couldn't listen without laughing.

The only situation that rivaled a high-pitched rendition of "How Great Thou Art" in terms of our trying to maintain composure was if this really sweet lady named Ruth showed up to sing alto in the choir. Ruth didn't sing as much as she bellowed, and when she'd chime in for the harmony on "Holy, Holy, Holy" or "Great Is Thy Faithfulness," Paige and I would pretty much have to crawl underneath the pews. In fact, there were times I nearly bit my tongue in half just trying to make it through one of Miss Ruth's impassioned choruses of "The Old Rugged Cross." It would lay me right out—and not because the Holy Spirit was having His way, either.

The pastor, who for most of my childhood was Dr. Pigott, would preach for twenty to twenty-five minutes, and if he went much past 11:45, people started getting antsy. If he preached long enough that the folks in the back row could hear the folks from the Baptist church across the street slamming car doors and driving past our sanctuary on the way to Sunday lunch, forget it. You have never seen an antsier bunch of congregants in your life.

(Sidenote: Now that I'm grown and have a pastor who regularly preaches for fifty-five to sixty minutes each week, I look back on those days of twenty-minute sermons and think, *BUCK UP, METHODISTS.*)

(However, my mother-in-law would want me to be sure to point out that if you're not out of church and in your car by noon, "You have to wait forever in line at lunch! Just forever! You really just have no idea how difficult it makes things! You'll wait forever!")

(I like to tease her and remind her that sometimes the Lord will put her in situations where she has to suffer for the sake of the gospel.)

(She doesn't find that nearly as funny as I do.)

After the sermon we'd sing another hymn, and then if new people were transferring membership or joining the church, we'd hear all about them from the pastor. Usually everybody would stay a little longer after the service to shake hands and make introductions and welcome the new members. By that point I was usually able to gauge Mama and Daddy's reaction about how well I'd behaved in church that day—and whether I'd be risking life and limb to ask about having a friend over that afternoon.

Then we'd all go home—until we met again for Family Night Supper on Wednesday.

And here's what strikes me about every bit of what I just told you.

That was my reality for the better part of ten years. Every single Sunday it was the same thing (barring an illness accompanied by fever or the occasional vacation). Every single Sunday I followed that same routine. And to this day, though I cannot recount the highlights from a single three-point sermon I heard at Mission Hill United Methodist Church—and I heard aplenty, as Papaw Davis would put it—I can say without hesitation that so much of what I know about mercy, about grace, about going to church and being the church . . . well, I learned it inside those walls.

I have to say: that's the neatest feeling, y'all.

And I've also heard enough of other people's stories about church to know that feeling is all too rare.

• • •

As I got older, I eased my way into Methodist Youth Fellowship and every possible junior high activity at church. We had a youth director who was THE MOST FUN (caps totally necessary), and he did the best job of making church a way of life, not just a destination on Sundays. He took us to every camp, every away football game, every "fellowship" weekend at the beach that he possibly could, and I know with everything in me that being part of that tight-knit group of guys and girls was a huge reason why junior high wasn't a painful or icky time for me. I mean, don't get me wrong: I WAS A GOOB. But I had plenty of equally goob-y friends, and I'm convinced that this is an oft-overlooked Key to Life: find other people who operate at your same level of nerdiness, and proceed with the rocking on.

Every October our church's eighth and ninth graders went to a place called Camp Wesley Pines for a weekend retreat. That eighth-grade trip marked the first time that I'd spent a weekend away from my parents, so clearly that was all kinds of major. I also had a big crush on one of the ninth-grade boys, but since I was way too shy around guys to flirt, I spent most of the weekend secretly giving Cute Boy the side eye while I mouthed the words to "El-Shaddai" and tried to make sure my hair looked good.

Clearly I had my priorities straight.

But in ninth grade, something about the weekend was different. I had just turned fourteen, after all, so there was the obvious wisdom that went along with that (just so you know, I'm rolling my eyes straight out of my head right now). But more than anything else, I found myself really listening to the speakers and worship leaders. I met a sweet friend named Mary Helen, and during the breaks we'd have long, rambling conversations about our hometowns, our churches, our families, and our schools. I wasn't focused on boys or drama or whether or not I sounded like Amy Grant when I'd try to imitate her raspy alto on "Sing Your Praise to the Lord." And for the first time in my life, I think, I made a choice that weekend to sit before the Lord and see what He had to say to me.

That Saturday night the worship leader presented the gospel. I can't say for sure that I understood all the ins and outs and whys and wherefores, but here's the part that I heard for sure:

You are a sinner.
God loves you anyway.
God sent His Son, Jesus, to bear the weight of your sins and die in your place.
Are you willing to lay down your life, take up your cross, and follow Him?

Somehow, in the midst of the off-key singing and the back-row giggling and the junior high fidgeting, I knew that my answer was yes.

Honestly, if I'd known how messy and broken and confused my heart would prove itself to be over the next ten or so years, I might have second-guessed my decision and said, "You know what, Lord? I don't think you want to fool with the likes of me."

But the call of the Lord was irresistible. That's kind of His deal, I reckon. And even though I was barely fourteen years old, there wasn't a doubt in my mind that something in my heart had shifted—even if I couldn't fully explain it. Jesus had met me right where I was, and while, oh have mercy, there were years of sifting and sanctification and surrender ahead of me, Camp Wesley Pines was the official starting point in my personal relationship with the Lord.

I'm still just as tickled as I can be that He wasn't put off by the fact that I was wearing a matching light-blue tracksuit and some pretty sweet white leather Converse tennis shoes.

He's obviously a smidge more holy than I am.

• • •

I spent most of my elementary school years singing in the Mission Hill children's choir under the direction of a lady named Miss Kitty Morris. Even though there were only about eight of us who regularly attended Sunday afternoon rehearsals, Miss Kitty was faithful to lead us. Her advancing years had left her stooped and wrestling with a mild case of palsy, but that didn't stop her from teaching us her favorites from a Methodist songbook that was ever present on top of the piano in the choir room. She'd sing along as we tried to learn the rhythm of "Pass It On," and whenever we'd get to the chorus of "Ten Thousand Angels," Miss Kitty would play the chords so loudly that we had to strain to hear ourselves sing the words:

> He could have called ten thousand angels
> To destroy the world and set Him free.
> He could have called ten thousand angels,
> But He died alone for you and me.

When I was around eight or nine years old, I thought Miss Kitty must like for that part to sound really dramatic. I couldn't see the significance in the way that she'd close her eyes and how she'd almost whisper those last two lines. I didn't know that Miss Kitty was leading us in *worship*, overcome by the gospel again and again.

There's something about the awareness of your own salvation that prompts you to see things with new eyes, and suddenly I was able to see a deeper layer to this place I already loved. And all the days when I walked the halls of the church, when I watched Miss Kitty lead us, when I showed up for Sunday school, when I listened to Bible stories, when I read the responsive readings, when I recited the creeds, when I listened to the choir, when I sang the hymns, and when I avoided Jell-O in all its forms at Family Night

Supper—well, after I put my trust in Jesus, I started to understand what all the fuss was about. By and large, people weren't showing up at church week after week because they didn't have anything better to do and because they got a kick out of seeing what everybody was wearing.

(I'll go ahead and confess right now that that Sunday Morning Fashion Watch is what carried me through the majority of church services during the first fourteen years of my life.)

(Okay. It has carried me through a few years since then too.)

But what I came to understand is that there was one reason and one reason alone that explained the faithfulness, the generosity, the compassion, the sincerity of the folks I had grown to love at Mission Hill.

Jesus.

It had been Him all along.

Only He could take a building filled with folding chairs and an old Coke machine and turn it into a kind of spiritual home. And only He could take a bunch of quirky people who otherwise might have only nodded hello to each other in the Winn-Dixie and turn them into brothers and sisters.

That just beats all, doesn't it?

CHAPTER 3

WHAT MISSISSIPPI DOES

She hugs you real tight and asks how your mama's doin'.
She remembers the best about you, forgets the worst, and forgives
even when you haven't asked.
She shops with her mama, her sisters, her daughters, and her nieces—
and she's always certain that they've never had more fun.
She listens.
She figures out what people you have in common, even if she has to
spend ten minutes asking questions about where your relatives
live—and then five more minutes making a phone call to a cousin
to see if the McWinns still own that house on 16th Avenue.
She tells you how darlin' you are and asks where in the world you got
your cute sweater.
She adores the names of her favorite small towns, places like
Noxapater, D'Lo, Arcola, and Itta Bena.

She knows that grace and mercy are so much better when they're shared.

She trusts that love is the better way.

She's there when you get married, when you have a baby, when one of your people dies, when your kids get baptized, and when you least expect it but need it the most.

She remembers your name.

She's well aware that the Lord gives and takes away, and she's at peace with that because, well, she figures He knows best.

She rocks babies, wipes noses, ties shoelaces, and sings "This Little Light of Mine" soft and low.

She makes a killer hash brown casserole.

She studies the Bible, reads Miss Welty, watches Bravo, and connects themes from all three while you're standing in the produce department at the Piggly Wiggly.

She creates artful arrangements for her dining room table with hydrangeas, privet, and some sticks from her backyard.

She keeps her commitments.

She tells her little girl that she needs to stand up for herself as she fastens a bow the size of a dinner plate in her hair.

She celebrates the birth of her first grandbaby and decides that she'd prefer to be called "Honey" or "Mimi" or "Sweetmama" from that day forward.

She keeps a secret stash of unsweetened tea in the back of the refrigerator just in case one of her guests is "off the sugar."

She wants more for you than you could ever want for yourself.

She always welcomes you home with wide-open arms.

And she asks when you'll be back again—with a sweet smile on her face—every single time you leave.

CHAPTER 4

REDEMPTION SOUNDS A LITTLE BIT LIKE AN OLD GEORGE JONES SONG

I AM A certified, bona fide, dyed-in-the-wool child of the seventies.

I didn't appreciate it at the time, of course. Kids rarely look around at the landscape of their youth and think, *Whoa. This is awesome! I'm so glad I am alive during this particular stretch of history!*

But looking back, I am oh-so-grateful—especially as a mama in the twenty-first century, where there's a tendency to bubble-wrap children as infants, add padding and armor for elementary school, and then unwrap them very gingerly when they turn eighteen.

If their delicate self-esteem can withstand this big, bad, mean ole world, of course.

(I'm really not trying to be critical.)

(We have an increasing tendency to make our kids very aware of their *specialness*.)

Back in the seventies, however, parents were less concerned about how kids felt and way more concerned that kids stayed out of their hair. Nobody had a clue about genetically modified organisms or the dangers of high-fructose corn syrup or the benefits of organic produce. You just ate your Cheetos and drank your Coke from a bottle and then topped off your snack with the recommended daily allowance of Pop Rocks.

That's why mamas in Myrtlewood were perfectly content to stand in the middle of the Winn-Dixie and visit while young'uns would run all over the store—sometimes without shoes. (To be clear, we did have shoes in Mississippi—OH GOOD GRIEF, AMERICA, I PROMISE—but sometimes in the summers we opted not to wear them because it was ONE HUNDRED AND SIXTY-TWO DEGREES outside.) If we exhausted our options in the grocery store, we'd walk to Howards Rexall or the T. G. & Y., both just down the sidewalk from the Winn-Dixie. Howards is where I first developed my love for browsing in drugstores; there was always something interesting to try (samples of Love's Baby Soft, anyone?). And Miss Maida, who worked there from the time that Moses was a child, always called me by name and asked how my parents were doing.

Once the grocery shopping was finished, mamas would round up the kids (sometimes by checking in with Miss Maida or a clerk at the T. G. & Y.), throw paper bags full of groceries in the backseat of a gigantic sedan with scorching-hot vinyl upholstery, and then instruct an older sibling to hold a younger sibling in the front seat on the way home so that the mama's hands were free to smoke a cigarette with the windows rolled up. It was usually just a matter of time before the younger kid would break free, crawl in the backseat, and lie down on top of the speakers in the back window. The mama wouldn't say anything because she was too busy listening to "Music Box Dancer" on the 8-track player while she flicked a succession of inch-long ashes in her car's convenient, built-in ashtray.

It was a simpler time.

And for me, the nonhelicopter vibe was in full force at home, too. My next-door neighbors and I rode go-carts without helmets, we ran around in the woods all by ourselves, and sometimes, when our parents needed to run errands, they'd tell us to hop in the bed of the pickup truck and tag along. You don't really see kids riding around in the beds of trucks anymore—I'm sure it's been proven too risky by four or nine government agencies—but back in the seventies our parents weren't walking around worried that something terrible was going to happen to us. They gave us a pretty wide berth of freedom.

One of my favorite perks of that wide berth (now there's a phrase I haven't once uttered since I waddled my way into a delivery room eleven years ago) was that I got to ride my bike pretty much anywhere I wanted. Granted, I wasn't going to go *too* far, because I was a little bit of a homebody and DISTANCE CYCLING, NO THANK YOU, but the bike enabled me to make the trek to my friend Kimberly's house if the weather was decent. There were about three miles that separated my house from hers, and even though there was a side road a little ways from my house that provided a detour from the bulk of the traffic, the last part of the bike route to the Clarks' house required me to ride my bike ACROSS A HIGHWAY—a fact that fills me with no small amount of fear and trepidation now that I'm a mama myself. All I can figure is that my parents were either totally laid back or totally tired. I'm guessing that it was more of the latter, but either way, there really were some good lessons from that level of independence.

(Even if I wasn't wearing any sort of protective headgear when I rode my bike ACROSS THE HIGHWAY.)

(AT THE AGE OF ELEVEN.)

(And fist bump to your parental courage, Mama and Daddy—you daredevil rascals, you.)

The Clarks lived in a charming Cape Cod–style house that basically looked like something out of a storybook. The white clapboard siding always stood out against the backdrop of trees behind the house, and the shutters were the perfect shade of magnolia-leaf green. In the midseventies, Kimberly's daddy decided that he was going to start a rose garden, so to the left of the driveway—beside the garage that looked more like a carriage house—there were at least twenty rosebushes. They'd start blooming in the spring and last through the early part of fall; it's almost impossible to think about their house without picturing that explosion of pink and yellow and coral blooms.

As an adult, I'm all too aware that roses can't grow like that—nothing can—unless there's some mighty fertile soil.

• • •

I honestly can't remember a time when the Clarks weren't a part of our extended family. When Kim's mother, Evelyn, was about twenty years old, she became friends with my mama, Ouida, and my mama's sister, Choxie. Evelyn and Choxie were actually roommates when they were single and working for a local bank; they rented the top floor in a house not too far from Myrtlewood's main park, and I can only imagine how sassy and stylish they must have been. In my mind they must have been just like Doris Day in *That Touch of Mink* or *Pillow Talk*: lots of pencil skirts, cropped jackets, modest heels, fur stoles, and pillbox hats. I picture them clocking out at the bank and going on a double date to one of Myrtlewood's better restaurants—a place where they'd order chopped steak and a baked potato, maybe some green beans in a bundle on the side—before they enjoyed lemon icebox pie and coffee for dessert.

(I have no idea why these completely pretend details are so important to me.)

(Apparently I am a person who needs a lot of concrete information. Even if I have to make it up.)

Mama and Daddy were already married when Evelyn and Choxie were rooming together; eventually Evelyn married Bill, and Choxie married Joe. The marriages only strengthened everybody's connections. Mama and Evelyn had their first children—both girls—within a year of each other, and well over a decade later, they both delivered what were considered "late in life" babies. That's when Kim and I arrived on the scene. I was born in October, and Kim was born the following March; Mama and Evelyn no doubt spent the next twelve to eighteen months commiserating about how exhausting it was to add another baby to the mix when you're almost forty.

Kim and I like to think that we kept 'em young.

They would probably beg to differ.

By the time Kim and I were old enough to ride our bikes to each other's houses, we were more like sisters than friends. Our families took trips together, shared meals together, and celebrated holidays together. Evelyn and Bill were the only two adults I got to call by their first names—no

"Mr." or "Mrs." required—and their house was almost as familiar to me as my own. I knew that their milk would always be in a glass bottle instead of a paper carton since Evelyn believed it tasted better that way. I knew that Bill kept his collection of Kenny Rogers and Dottie West country music albums inside a console in their dining room. I knew that Evelyn's tuna salad was way better than Mama's because Evelyn didn't put chopped celery or apples in hers. I knew that Bill would always play baseball with us if we begged him long enough—and I knew that after the game Evelyn would serve us iced tea so sweet that it might qualify as syrup. I knew that they kept the Planters peanuts and Reese's Peanut Butter Cups in the kitchen cabinets to the left of the stove, just below the spot where Bill kept his cartons of Benson & Hedges 100s and Evelyn kept her cartons of Virginia Slims Lights.

(By the way, I just looked up a picture of an old Virginia Slims ad so that I could make sure I had the brand right.)

(The ad features a woman who is wearing tennis clothes—and holding a lit cigarette.)

(Apparently the early eighties were a time when physical exercise and cigarette smoking were not considered contradictory activities.)

(Game, set, match—and *smoke, y'all.*)

• • •

Evelyn and Bill were both hysterical—quick witted, fun loving, and easygoing. They loved to laugh with Kim and me, and from a young age, I noticed that even my parents laughed more when the Clarks were around. Their house was the site of all manner of celebrations—birthdays, New Year's Eves, Friday night dinners—and I guess that sort of leads us to the next thing I knew about their house, though at the time it was not nearly as significant to me as the location of the Reese's Peanut Butter Cups: at the Clarks' there was always a jug of Paul Masson Chablis in the refrigerator (and I don't mean bottle—I mean JUG)—along with six or twelve Old Milwaukee beers. It didn't seem like that big of a deal, really; it was just part and parcel of being at their house.

Sure, Evelyn and Bill drank more than my parents did, but that wasn't necessarily saying much. Mama has always contended that she's allergic to alcohol (I know. You just have to take her word for it and move on.), and while Daddy enjoys an occasional glass of wine, he has always been way too self-disciplined to habitually indulge in anything. In fact, Daddy's commitment to sensible, upright living prompted Bill to give him a nickname that has stuck for more than fifty years: "The Reverend."

Bill's high regard for nicknames was a source of endless entertainment to all of us. If he loved you, he refused to call you by your given name, which is why Kim was Kimber or KC (and the Sunshine Band), her sister Margaret was Mae, my sister was Suza, Mama was Sugah (not sugar—SUGAH), Choxie was Choxah—I could write a list so long that you'd need a scroll to contain it. Even the Clarks' cat, Pizitz, had a nickname: LePew.

And just in case you're wondering, my nickname was Soap. For a while, at least. Because when my friends christened me with the nickname "Sofa" in high school, Bill followed suit with his own name for me.

He always liked to be on track with the trends.

I never really analyzed why I loved being at the Clarks' house so much—I didn't have a big need to escape life at my own house—but I imagine that part of it was that Bill's outgoing personality guaranteed there was always something extra fun going on. Plus, since Evelyn and Bill were like second parents, they treated me like one of their own. Bill couldn't carry a tune in a bucket but would serenade Kim and me with the song of our choosing whenever we asked. Evelyn let us play in her makeup and dress up in her clothes, and if Kim and I got a wild hair at ten o'clock at night and decided to bake brownies or cookies, Evelyn would stay up with us, rocking in her chair by the kitchen fireplace while she read her latest Harlequin Romance and simultaneously put the hurt on a pack of those aforementioned Virginia Slims Lights. Evelyn and Bill both loved Password, Sorry!, and gin rummy, and the four of us spent countless nights playing games on the floor in their den.

I wasn't related to them. Not even a little bit.

But they were family.

And it occurs to me that God has a mysterious way of giving us homes in places where we don't necessarily have an official return address.

• • •

It's funny, because when you're a kid, you don't really have an awareness of other people's brokenness. I guess it's because you don't really have an understanding of your own. And from the time we were six until we were about ten, I'd say that Kim and I had a pretty carefree go of things. We considered a sleepover a total success if we got to slide down her stairs a bunch of times and play sisters for several hours.

(My pretend name was Holly.)

(I worked in a pretend clothing store.)

(My pretend boyfriend's name was Scott.)

(As in Baio.)

We also liked to play Bill's favorite country albums and pretend like we were competing in pageants as we belted out the most dramatic songs we could find. Evelyn's heaviest glass candlesticks were our microphones, and there were several country hits in our repertoire: "Louisiana Woman, Mississippi Man," "(Hey Won't You Play) Another Somebody Done Somebody Wrong Song," and "Don't Come Home A' Drinkin' (with Lovin' on Your Mind)," to name a few.

You should know that the subtext of those songs was completely lost on us. Plus, it never really occurred to us that no one had ever been crowned Miss Mississippi after singing a song about adultery during the talent competition.

But somewhere in between the time when I started riding my bike to the Clarks' house and the time when I started driving, something changed. The best way I know to explain it is that there were glimpses of brokenness I hadn't noticed before, even if I wasn't exactly sure how to label it. Maybe part of the reason was because Kim and I were getting older and were a little more aware of what our expectations were in terms of "normal" behavior from our parents, but there was no question that Bill's drinking had escalated—and there wasn't much about it that seemed "social" anymore.

In the summers I spent most Mondays with Kim; it was Bill's day off, and since the Clarks had more cable channels than we did (plus Atari!), Kim and I tended to gravitate to her house instead of mine. Most of those

Mondays have blurred together as sort of a collective happy memory, but there's one that was a watershed moment for both of us, I think.

One Monday when Kim and I were twelve, Bill asked us if we'd ride with him to the store—in his sah-weet green Camaro, no less. I thought that I'd seen him drinking earlier in the day—I wasn't completely sure—but I figured it was safe to get in the car with him (keep in mind: I was twelve; plus, Kim and I always loved riding around in that Camaro). But about a half a mile from their house, I realized that something was wrong. And no matter how many jokes he cracked, no matter how loud he turned up the radio so we could sing along, no matter how fun and carefree I tried to pretend like the car ride was, there was no denying that he was drunk. Not tipsy. Not buzzed. Drunk.

It was the first time his drinking had ever made me feel scared.

And sometimes, when I think about Kim and me in the backseat of that car, trying our best to find something to laugh about as we swerved back and forth along the road, my heart hurts a little bit. When he was sober, Bill would have never dreamed of doing anything to put us in danger; he looked after us and tended to us and loved us like crazy. Kim was his beloved, brilliant baby girl, and it was his great joy to dote on her. He thought she was the absolute best at everything she tried, whether it was ballet, piano, flute, or tap dancing; no daddy could love a daughter more. In fact, one time when Kim accidentally pinned Evelyn between her car and the garage door (it's a long story), Bill was so worried about Kim's emotional state after the accident that he bought her a purse. Evelyn used to laugh and say that if Kim had actually succeeded in injuring her, there's no question that Bill would have bought her a new piece of luggage.

But that's what stinks about the parts of us that are broken and hurting. We try our best to keep all the pieces and shards gathered and contained, and we trick ourselves into thinking that they're not affecting other people. Eventually, though, our need to feed what is broken starts to overpower everything else, and those hurting places make us careless and reckless. Before we know it—and sometimes after it's too late—we look around and see that the people we love the most have been wounded in the collateral damage.

And listen. I certainly don't mean to imply that my own family was so full of awesomeness that I had to go visit somewhere to see some dysfunction at work. Heavens, no. But the thing about your own family's dysfunction is that typically you're so immersed in it that you don't always see it for what it is. When you're with someone else's family, though, you haven't spent a lifetime conditioning yourself to look past the unhealthier stuff.

(That last paragraph sounds like I have somehow confused myself with Dr. Phil.)

(I do apologize.)

(All those psychology classes that I took in college just ROSE UP AND DEMANDED TO SPEAK.)

• • •

Now. As a bit of a history lesson for the young people, I will point out that before there was any such thing as a cell phone, people had to call each other on a telephone that was connected to all the other phones in the house. What this meant was that your privacy extended only as far as your parents allowed it, and also, your parents did not care one iota about your privacy. They could pick up the phone at any second and (1) listen in on your conversations, (2) tell you to get off the phone, or (3) some combination of 1 and 2.

Maybe that's why one particular phone call from Kim stands out so much in my memory. I was a sophomore in high school, and she was a freshman, and one Wednesday night she called and asked if I could come over right away. At the time the driving age was fifteen in Mississippi, and please know that now that I am an adult, I share in your early driving-age horror. Anyway, I was standing in the kitchen when she called, and as I started to respond to her story, the tone of my voice got my mama's attention. Mama stopped cleaning up the kitchen, and as I tried to create some privacy by stretching the phone cord into the dining room (Here's another fun fact, kids: phones had cords. And the only people who had phones in their cars were detectives on TV shows.), Mama followed me step for step. Her maternal radar was pinging like crazy—and for mighty good reason.

It took Kim all of about fourteen seconds to break the news: Bill had gone to rehab.

Keep in mind that back then the whole idea of rehab (or "treatment," as some people called it) was mysterious and vague—something that seemed reserved for rock stars or characters on *ABC Afterschool Specials*. I don't think I'd ever known anyone in real life who had gone away to deal with an addiction.

But that night on the phone, Kim told me how a series of events had convinced Bill that he couldn't get better on his own. Bill finally realized that he was desperate for some intervention. Evelyn had driven him to Jackson late that afternoon, and since she wouldn't be home until very late that night, Kim called to see if I could spend the night so she wouldn't be by herself while she waited for her mama.

Of course my parents said yes—they didn't want Kim to be alone and understood why she wanted to be at her own house—so I hopped in my burnt sienna 1978 Chevrolet Impala (jealous much?) and drove those three miles that I'd traveled hundreds of times before.

Everything was the same.

Everything was different.

• • •

If the *Afterschool Specials* had prepared me for anything, it was that my time at Kim's house that night was going to be filled with all manner of earnest conversation. Kim had never been much of a crier, so I didn't really anticipate that there would be tears, but I imagined that she'd need some encouragement. I felt certain that I would need to comfort her with some very deep thoughts—perhaps even a brief reading from the Psalms.

Oh, I was going to Be There for Her. Yes, I was.

But once I walked into Kim's house and we worked through a few initially awkward moments of "So, how about that rehab business?" it became crystal clear that there was one very valuable lesson that the *Afterschool Specials* hadn't taught me: when a loved one finally acknowledges a struggle and bravely asks for help, it feels like *relief* more than anything else. It feels like *hope*. That doesn't mean that there won't be uncertainty and difficulty in the process, but, oh have mercy, there is the most glorious reality in the wake of it all: it is *forward progress*.

Kim and I didn't say that out loud, of course. We were fourteen and fifteen years old, for heaven's sake. What we said out loud was more along the lines of this:

"So, are you, like, *okay*? Because we can, like, go to, like, Wendy's, and get, like, a Frosty if you're not."

"Like, I think I'm fine? Because I'm, like, *sad*, but, like, in a good way, you know?"

Feel free to memorize our conversation so that you can call it to mind when you're in a situation where you need to offer someone a little encouragement.

We ended up not going to Wendy's after all. I had a poetry portfolio due in English the next day, so I really needed to manufacture some Deep Thoughts and then put them to paper in the form of loosely connected sentence fragments. Kim couldn't get the Prince song "4 the Tears in Your Eyes" out of her head (it was 1985, y'all) (Prince was epic), and eventually we started making up motions to the lyrics.

Long ago, there was a man
Change stone to bread with the touch of his hand
Made the blind see and the dumb understand
He died for the tears in your eyes.

I mean, it wasn't a John Wesley hymn or anything, but now that I think about it, it sure did put the focus where focus was due.

Everything was different.

Everything was the same.

• • •

Two months later, Bill came home.

There are a lot of details about his recovery that I've never known. I don't know why he started drinking. I don't know when he realized that he had a problem. I don't know why it got worse when it did. I don't know what ultimately convinced him that he needed to stop.

But I know enough about my own brokenness to understand that sometimes you just get to the end of your dadgum self. Those parts of our hearts and lives that try to live in perpetual exile—well, eventually it's almost like they long to be reconciled. They want to be whole.

And when Bill came home, his inner transformation was so profound that it was outwardly visible. I'll never forget it. He and Evelyn stopped by Mama and Daddy's the day after he completed his treatment, and he looked like a new man. I mean, I get that it might sound kind of strange for me to say that he glowed, but yes. *That.* He looked healthy, vibrant, and alive. More than anything else, I remember his eyes: clear, steady, and crystal blue. Whatever used to blur his vision was a thing of the past.

The memory of that day reminds me of Paul's exhortation at the end of 2 Corinthians: "Brothers and sisters, rejoice! Strive for full restoration, encourage one another, be of one mind, live in peace. And the God of love and peace will be with you" (13:11, NIV). I didn't know it at the time— I was fifteen, after all—but now I can see so clearly that as Mama and Daddy wrapped their arms around their friend of more than thirty years, as they laughed and cried and celebrated, as Bill shared what the Lord had done in his life, I witnessed Paul's words in action. Live and in person.

The God of love and peace filled Mama and Daddy's den that afternoon. And He was beautiful.

• • •

Bill's recovery changed his life—no doubt about it. But here's the part that continues to preach to me even now, thirty years later: his recovery also established a redemptive legacy for his children and grandchildren. In fact, just a few weeks ago Kim texted me a picture of her daughter, Anna Clair, who was all dressed up for a Christmas dance, and I did an honest-to-goodness double take when I clicked on the picture.

Kim's brilliant, beautiful firstborn is now fourteen—the same age that her mama was when Bill went to rehab and I drove that 1978 Chevrolet Impala over to the Clarks' with every intention of reading some psalms aloud. I stared at Anna Clair's picture for almost a full minute, and after I marveled at how she somehow resembles Bill and Evelyn and Kim and Kim's husband all at the same time, I was overcome by what a privilege it has been to see redemption at work over the course of three generations, to watch a stronghold gradually loosen its grip and then disappear altogether.

I mean, I kind of thought the biggest perk of hanging out at the Clarks' house was the unlimited supply of Reese's, but it turns out that grace had a way bigger story to tell.

There's an old George Jones song that always reminds me of Bill; I'm certain that if it had been around in the seventies or eighties, Bill would have added it to his record collection in the dining room console. Like so much country music, the song tells a tale of heartache and a second chance (you'll be relieved to know that no one's dog dies, and there's not a single mention of tractors or trucks)—and I think Bill, like so many of us, would be able to relate. Granted, Bill wouldn't necessarily be singing to one of George Jones's wives, but I can't help but think there's Someone to whom these lyrics would apply.

All it took was your sweet love
To rise above it all
You can build 'em strong and tall
But walls can fall

Oh, listen. I know with everything in me that Kim and I would have gotten such a kick out of hearing her daddy sing those words.

Granted, he might not have been able to carry a tune in a bucket.

But his song would have been more beautiful than ever before.

CHAPTER 5

TWENTY-SIX ACTIVITIES OF GREAT SUBSTANCE THAT I ENJOYED IN HIGH SCHOOL

1. Rolling my hair with Conair Hot Sticks because VOLUME.
2. Watching *Moonlighting*.
3. Reading anything I could find about *Moonlighting*.
4. Putting way too much emphasis on *Moonlighting*.
5. Trying to create some serious boy drama in my life despite the fact that I didn't actually, you know, *date* anyone.
6. Offering to say the prayer at Methodist Youth Fellowship on Sunday nights so nobody would forget that I was a good little church girl.
7. Wondering what all the Jesus stuff meant outside of being a good little church girl.
8. Riding around singing along with Amy Grant's *The Collection* with my friends Elizabeth and Marion.

9. Believing with everything in me that no matter what problems I faced, AMY GRANT UNDERSTOOD THEM.
10. Choreographing ballet routines to the sound track from *St. Elmo's Fire* in order to artistically convey all my Very Deep Emotions.
11. Stopping at the Jitney Jr. on the way home from school to buy a bag of O'Grady's Au Gratin potato chips and a Mello Yello.
12. Trying to figure out why I couldn't seem to get rid of an extra twenty pounds and never really making the whole O'Grady's Au Gratin/Mello Yello connection.
13. Nodding my head a lot in sophomore year Honors Algebra II so nobody would pick up on the fact that I had no idea what was going on.
14. Going back to a regular math class my junior year because all that nodding I did in Honors Algebra II didn't really help me pass any tests.
15. Writing excruciatingly heartfelt journal entries in which I told myself all my problems.
16. Watching *SNL* over and over with my friend Ricky and laughing until I wheezed.
17. Considering the possibility that Phil Collins really *could* see the deepest parts of my heart.
18. Singing along to the Violent Femmes cassette with my friend Amanda and feeling super-alternative in my Esprit sweater, Guess? jeans, and Tretorn tennis shoes.
19. Reading epic, hilarious notes from my friend Joni—and working *really* hard to respond with a note that would make her laugh just as much.
20. Screaming "Clang, clang, clang went the trolley"—and all the other lines from Sweeney Sisters' medleys—with Elizabeth.
21. Putting on a pair of high-waisted jeans, looking in a mirror, and marveling at how flattering they were.
22. Living in a state of delusion about that whole "flattering high-waisted jeans" thing.
23. Writing superlong letters to my out-of-town buddies Meg and

Mary Helen. (Dear kids of the twenty-first century, I realize that this concept of "writing letters" might be unfamiliar to you, but it was what we had to do to communicate with people who didn't live in our town because there was no such thing as texting, and calling someone long-distance wasn't terribly affordable for the teenage set.)

24. Staring at pretty much any passage from the Old Testament and thinking, *Well, what's that got to do with anything?*

25. Perfecting my use of royal-blue mascara.

26. Clinging to the hope I saw in Ephesians 3:20-21—but secretly doubting if it really applied to me.

Yeah. I know that last one is kinda serious.

But I went to college with some real-live questions, y'all.

And part of me kept hoping that Amy Grant would show up to answer them.

CHAPTER 6

THE LESSER-KNOWN OBJECTIVES
OF HIGHER EDUCATION

I HADN'T BEEN at college very long at all when I decided that the keys to a successful freshman year were really quite simple: a cute dorm room, access to good fried chicken, and a tan.

I know. You're thinking, *Gosh, that all sounds a little superficial.*

And you are so right about that.

But the bigger pieces of the puzzle—friends and school—seemed to be fitting into place just fine, so I felt free to examine what could be considered a *subset* of that success criteria.

I know. You're thinking, *But, um, isn't the God-size piece of that puzzle the most important of all?*

And you are so right about that.

But college was the first time in my whole life when nobody was looking from the choir loft to see if I was at church on Sunday mornings. So I wasn't exactly, um, *prioritizing* my spiritual life, unless you count my sporadic reading of Charles Swindoll's *Growing Strong in the Seasons of Life*.

I liked to tell myself that skimming a devotional book once every two or four months was totally keeping my Jesus tank filled to overflowing.

Also: *I was a fool.*

Really, when I look back on it, the cute-dorm-room thing was pretty much under control. My roommate, Amanda, and I had picked out peach-and-green comforters the summer before we left for Mississippi State, and her mama, who is a fantastic seamstress, created an adorable assortment of floral throw pillows that coordinated with the comforters. I even drove to Starkville about a month before school started so that I could STENCIL PAINT THE WALLS IN OUR DORM ROOM—a clear sign that I'd read one too many of Mama's *Country Living* magazines and maybe set some overly ambitious decorating goals.

Nonetheless, Amanda and I had a darling room (I always feel like putting a *g* on the end of that word is a complete betrayal of my Mississippi roots, but I'm gonna run with it). We managed to decorate around the giant desk that dominated the center of our living area, and we even elevated our beds so that we'd have some much-needed storage for sweaters, books, and in my case, Dr Pepper (my Diet Coke addiction wouldn't take hold for several more years). It didn't take long to think of our tiny shared space as home. And when I'd finish a hard day of classes (Oh, who am I kidding? I was an English major, which means that I spent the better part of each day in humanities classes, aka Let's Talk About All of Our Feelings.), I couldn't wait to get back to Critz 218 and walk into our little room.

The only hitch in my dorm-room giddy-up was that Amanda was a very organized and self-disciplined engineering major, and as a result she did things like "attend class regularly" and "study every afternoon" and "get plenty of rest." My own personal academic strategy was a bit less rigorous, to say the least (please see "talking about the feelings"). And since Amanda liked to go to bed early, I developed a routine that I followed to the letter almost every night: I'd put on my pajamas, grab whatever book I was reading, make sure I had a notebook and a pen, drag our phone out in the hall-way, and then sit cross-legged against the wall outside our door. I eventually came to think of that space as my office, and if my friends wanted to find me, that was the first place they'd look.

I wrote many a letter and called many a friend while sitting in that hallway—and I met a few folks too. Friends would come by with dates and study partners they'd signed into the dorm; girls from my hall would escort parents and siblings and cousins to their rooms. I connected all sorts of relational dots while I sat outside my door—which girls were from the same hometown, which girl had a crush on a guy from history class, which mama was having a hard time with her baby being off at college—and in a weird way, the routine of it made me feel at home.

Go figure, huh?

• • •

I'd been at State about a month when I decided that I was going to step out of my comfort zone and stay on campus during an away-game weekend. Since most students at big Southern schools make their fall travel plans based on where the football team is playing, away games are usually a good opportunity to go home. However, that particular weekend I needed to work on a paper, and I figured I had better odds of being productive if I was stuck in my dorm room instead of visiting my hometown, where I'd no doubt alternate between hanging out with my high school friends and sleeping like I was getting paid for it.

So I stayed in Starkville.

After I'd worked on my paper for a couple of hours that Friday night, I started getting restless. Amanda and I didn't have cable in our dorm room, so other than a couple of fuzzy local channels, I couldn't watch TV, and even though a few people on my hall had also stayed on campus that weekend, they all seemed to have plans that didn't involve a freshman composition paper. Eventually I decided to walk to the other wing of the dorm and see if I anyone I knew was around.

To my credit, I do believe that I changed out of my Chi O nightshirt before I made my pilgrimage.

I mean, if you're going to walk around a dorm, wearing pants is typically a solid choice.

I didn't see a living soul until I got up to the third floor, where I noticed that a familiar-ish door was partially open. I'd talked with Elise and Tracey, the girls who lived there, on several different occasions since we were in the same sorority pledge class, but we hadn't hung out much because, well, there were a lot of girls in our pledge class, and in the grand scheme of things, there hadn't been that much time to get to know each other yet.

Since the door was cracked, I pushed on it as I knocked, and I immediately saw Elise making short order of a large pile of clean clothes. By the end of that year I would come to know that Elise tackles laundry like she's working on an assembly line. All business. If you interrupt the process, you do so at your peril. But that night, as she folded towel after towel with factory-level precision, I was kind of astounded by her folding focus, and after a couple of minutes I figured out that the best way to "help" would be to have a seat on Tracey's bed and stay out of Elise's way. That is precisely what I did—and we started to talk.

I very quickly learned three key bits of information about the semi-stranger who was folding her towels with such enthusiasm.

1. She was hilarious.
2. She was opinionated.
3. She was most hilarious when she was sharing her opinions.

And listen. I think it's safe to say that in Elise's dorm room that night, we forged a forever friendship. We laughed until we hurt—until we fell over and held our sides and fought to breathe—and by the time I left her room, I had a sneaking suspicion that no matter what our college years had in store for us, we'd figure out a way to laugh our way through it.

And that—*that* is what brings me to fried chicken.

You're just going to have to trust me with my unconventional transition.

Somewhere in my conversation with Elise that Friday night, we discovered our mutual affinity for fried chicken. Now, if you don't live in the Southern part of the country, you might wonder why the whole fried chicken thing would create such a Bonding Moment, but I would venture to say that it's one of the deepest sources of instant connection in the South.

Sure, there's a *general* appreciation for fried chicken that runs all through the culture down here, but when you find someone else who really *loves* it, there's so much more to explore: white meat vs. dark meat, buttermilk-soaked vs. brined, extra crispy vs. regular crust, mild seasonings vs. spicy.

(I daresay that more than a few marriages have teetered on the brink after a disagreement about extra crispy vs. regular crust. It's a divisive issue in this part of the country.)

(I'm convinced that it's a topic that should be covered in premarital counseling sessions.)

Anyway, Elise and I wasted no time discussing our fried chicken favorites, and when I mentioned that I really liked the fried chicken in State's cafeteria, Elise frowned a bit and said, "Really? Because I just don't see any way that it could top Popeyes."

"You like Popeyes that much?" I replied.

Oh.

Bless my heart.

Just typing that makes me want to travel back in time and pat my seventeen-year-old self on the head. Because I didn't know, y'all. *I just didn't know.*

This is probably a good time to clarify that in the central part of Mississippi where I grew up, we were undiscipled in the wonders of Popeyes Louisiana Kitchen at that particular point in time. Elise, however, was from south Mississippi and therefore close enough to New Orleans to have some legitimate fried chicken sense. I'd tried Popeyes, of course; I have a pretty vivid memory of being on Canal Street with my parents after my freshman year of high school and stepping into a Popeyes at lunchtime. I thought it was good, but I didn't really get it; I can only blame this reaction on the fact that a fourteen-year-old's fried chicken palate is oftentimes unsophisticated and unrefined.

You might say that my fried chicken sanctification was nowhere near complete.

That's why the Lord was so kind to send a friend like Elise for such a time as that. Because as Elise and I visited that fateful Friday night in her dorm room, I learned a lot about her; for example, she liked to call her parents "Cindy" and "Frank," her grandmother called her "Essie," she had been going out with a cute boy from the Delta named Paul, and she tended to brace her arms against the nearest door/wall/bedpost/available structure when she laughed.

But more than anything else, I learned that GIRLFRIEND KNOWS HER SOME GOOD FRIED CHICKEN.

No kidding. The very next day I went to Popeyes for lunch, and I'm so relieved to tell you that my seventeen-year-old self was able to fully appreciate what my fourteen-year-old self had not. I have never been the same.

By the grace of God, I have never been the same.

Interestingly enough, Elise has since shifted her fried chicken loyalties to Church's, but fortunately our friendship hasn't suffered for one second despite the difference in our fried chicken preferences.

There's no need to get bogged down in matters of Christian liberty, now is there?

So with the fried chicken part of the college equation settled (and, just for the record, it was settled definitively by the two-piece all-white Popeyes dinner, spicy, with a side of red beans and rice and a Dr Pepper), that only left one more freshman-year objective on the personal front: a tan.

• • •

It's probably important to point out that the sun and I have a long and complex history. From my perspective, a giant part of that history is that THE SUN HATES ME, but that might not be entirely fair. I've just had a lot of really bad sunburns over the course of my life—most accidental, some the result of pure-dee stupidity—so any situation where I'm actually *in* the sun tends to feel like it's fraught with peril and angst. It's better now that I'm older and have come to terms that I cannot walk outside my house unless I'm wearing a sunscreen with SPF in the double digits, but back in my college days, the sun and I had not yet made our peace with each other.

That didn't do a single thing to diminish my deep and consuming desire to look like someone in a Hawaiian Tropic ad.

Now if you have ever seen me in real life, you can attest to the fact that the good Lord did not make me with tanning in mind. As best I can remember, my hair is naturally dark blonde (thanks to Carla, my hair-dresser, it's been a while since I've seen my hair in its natural state), and my eyes are light blue. For the longest time I was convinced that I didn't have a trace of melanin in my skin, but about four years ago I realized that I could in fact turn sort of a muted pink after spending about thirty consecutive days at the pool while slathered in sunblock.

But my freshman year of college, I was still harboring some misguided notions that with a little planning, the perfect tan was within my reach. During the fall and winter I had no problem putting my sun-kissed dreams on the back burner, so to speak, but I never let go of the dream that once spring arrived, it was going to be my time to be tan.

Delusion is a powerful thing, my friends.

It didn't help that Elise, Tracey, Daph, Marion, and so many other folks seemed to tan with little to no effort. They could sit outside at the Chi O house on a sunny afternoon and look like they'd spent the weekend in the Caribbean. On top of that, they didn't burn at all—a feat that was utterly inconceivable to someone (um, ME) who once spent the majority of a van ride from Panama City to Myrtlewood vomiting repeatedly after a particularly wicked case of sun poisoning.

I was young and stupid. I had no idea that those UV rays poking through the clouds were the most dangerous rays of all.

• • •

By the time March of my freshman year rolled around, I was more con-vinced than ever that a tan was in my immediate future. Sigma Chi's annual Derby Day was fast approaching, and I knew it was going to force my tanning hand. My sorority was wearing red T-shirts, and someone who was clearly much tanner than I had decided that we needed to pair the red shirts with white shorts. Suffice it to say that fear and trembling filled my soul, because when you are melanin deficient (that is not an official term, but it sounds almost troubling, doesn't it?), white shorts are perhaps the most unflattering garment that you could dream of wearing against your glow-in-the-dark legs.

Honestly, the only positive thing I could come up with as far as the white shorts were concerned was that my veins would have never looked bluer.

So, since I didn't have the power to fight the sorority dress code, I figured I needed to be proactive and, you know, finally make a trip to a tanning bed. Oh, I could have settled for some self-tanner, but it was the late eighties, and the only thing self-tanner did, at least for me, was tint my skin an orangish hue that could not, be found in nature. To my way of thinking, the tanning bed was my only choice.

The day before Derby Day, I made an appointment with a local salon that had five or six tanning beds, and a couple of hours later, I drove across Starkville so I could meet my tanning destiny out on Highway 25. Unbeknownst to me, some beds had stronger bulbs than others, but since I didn't know that, I just picked the one with the cutest name and ended up in a bed called Bora-Bora.

Perhaps that should have been my first warning sign.

In hindsight, there are many things I wish I'd done differently. I wish I hadn't felt the pressure to be tan. I wish I hadn't waited until the day before Derby Day to start the tanning process. I wish I hadn't ignored my mama's many sun-related warnings that were blaring like weather alerts inside my head.

And more than anything, I wish I hadn't forgotten to put on sunscreen before I got in the tanning bed.

You see, it never occurred to me that stepping into a tanning bed without some sort of sunscreen was pretty much the equivalent of stepping onto a beach at noon (practically nude, mind you), slathering myself in Crisco, and staying put for three hours. All I can figure is that somewhere along the line I'd been deceived by the misnomer "*tanning* bed," because frankly, in my case, it should have been called a "burn-up-your-milky-white-behind bed."

But I'm getting ahead of myself.

After I'd spent about seventeen minutes in Bora-Bora, I decided I'd forfeit the last thirteen minutes of my appointment because, quite frankly, I was ready to go home. I was burning slap up (and I've never really been one to enjoy activities that involve heat), so I got out of the tanning bed, put on my clothes, and drove back to my dorm. I looked forward to the golden tan that would no doubt greet me the next morning, and I felt utterly relieved that I wasn't going to feel self-conscious wearing those bright-white shorts.

Life had never been so full of hope and promise.

But when morning came, there was no tan. I figured I hadn't stayed in Bora-Bora long enough, and I was just as sad about wasting fifteen dollars as I was that my legs were the same pasty white they'd been the day before. I gloomily donned my white shorts and red T-shirt, and even now I remember standing on the steps of the Chi O house as we prepared to walk over to Derby Day, hoping with everything in me that my perma-pale state wouldn't be an embarrassment to the sisterhood. Everybody else, at least in my estimation, seemed to have beautiful golden tans.

I, on the other hand, looked like Casper wearing a bright-red T-shirt.

The day was relatively uneventful, but after a couple of hours I definitely started to notice that my face felt flush. I chalked it up to all the Derby-ish excitement and didn't pay much attention until around tug-of-war time, when I also started to notice that my legs felt just the tiniest bit warm. The color of my skin started to make a gradual progression, too, and when the Derby Day festivities were over, I realized that my normal chalky whiteness had turned bright pink. About thirty minutes later, when I was back at the sorority house, I looked in a mirror, and I couldn't help but notice that I was beginning to look, well, *red*.

And by the time I got back to my dorm room, I was, you might say, *ablaze* with color.

I had plans to go out that night with my friend Bryan, who at the time drove an SUV. The primary reason this detail stands out so prominently in my memory is because when he picked me up, I had to climb into and out of the passenger seat, and I was all too aware that my knees were increasingly reluctant to do any sort of bending. We had a perfectly lovely time, as I recall, and I reckon it was a mighty good thing, because by the time he dropped me off at my dorm later that night, I knew that I was in capital-*T* Trouble.

Bora-Bora bit back, my friends.

And hard.

At first there was the nausea, and after a couple of hours of willing it to stop, I finally surrendered and went down the hall to the community bathroom, where I lay down and even slept a bit (I am mortified by every detail in the last half of this sentence). The unexpected bonus to dozing off in the bathroom was that the tile provided some sweet relief—because I cannot tell you how burning-up hot I was. I rubbed Noxzema over every part of my body, and I don't even care what kind of mental image that conjures, because OH, I was on fire with the heat of a thousand suns.

Or a thousand tanning bed bulbs, as it were.

But as it turned out, Saturday night was the easy part. Because Sunday was a full-on, sun-scorched plague.

By late Sunday afternoon, you see, the backs of my knees had started to blister and also ooze. As a result, I could not bend my knees at all, and that presented a bit of a problem in a collegiate setting where there are many, many stairs. I will never forget that I had a history test coming up that Monday morning, and since I didn't feel like I could contact my professor and tell him that I would be unable to take his test due to an unfortunate run-in with an evil tanning bed named Bora-Bora, I figured I could at least study with a friend of mine who was very smart and always took notes in class. She lived across campus, though, so I had no choice but to drive to her dorm (lowering myself into my Buick Regal was no easy feat), hobble across her parking lot, and then walk up several flights of stairs to get to her room.

All without bending my knees.

Honest to goodness, it took me twenty-five minutes to walk from the parking lot of McKee dorm up to the "intensive study floor" where my smart friend lived, and when I got there, I couldn't sit down because, well, BLISTERS ON BACKS OF KNEES, and I figured the resulting high-pitched scream might disturb the other residents. Unfortunately, after I stood around very awkwardly for several minutes, I realized that my "study buddy" was slightly annoyed by the prospect of helping me. Apparently she resented the fact that I had "skipped class" and "not taken notes," and I could not persuade her to have sympathy on me even though I could not, in fact, bend my knees. So at some point I just gave up and walked, stiff-legged, back down to my car. Once I actually made it to the car, I had to slide under the steering wheel with the seat pushed back as far as it would go because there was no way—no way at all—that my knees were Ever. Going. To. Bend. Again.

Make no mistake: they were JACKED UP.

Fortunately, I did get better over the course of the next few days. By the next week, I even attempted to roller-skate at a Chi O skating party. It was fun, but it wasn't necessarily a *wise* decision; when I fell, the scabs on the backs of my knees prevented me from getting up, and Elise's boyfriend, Paul, finally just let me hold on to his waist while he propelled me around the skating rink. Eventually I learned that if I needed to stop, I could hurl myself into the waist-level wall, and it would break my fall.

These—these are precious memories, aren't they?

I haven't even told you the part about how the scabs over the water blisters leaked a time or nine while I skated, so my jeans were covered with blistery liquid all across the backs of the knees.

Really, I don't know why I didn't come away from that event with several potential suitors.

I can't imagine that I've ever looked more attractive.

However, you'll be happy to know that when I was on the way home from the skating party, I stopped at the Popeyes and bought myself a delicious two-piece dinner. And when I got back home, I changed into my Chi O nightshirt before I coated my hot-pink legs in Noxzema, devoured my fried chicken, and admired the cuteness of my dorm room.

Sometimes, I guess, all your dreams really do come true.

CHAPTER 7

BECAUSE CONVERSATION, CHIPS, AND QUESO CAN FLAT-OUT BUILD A BRIDGE

ONE OF THE unusual parts about being the baby of the family by a ten-year margin was that by the time I was eight, my brother and my sister had already moved out of the house. It never felt strange to me, though. Being the baby by a mile was totally normal because it was all I'd ever known, but that didn't change the fact that sometimes the contrasts between our lives were almost comical. I was still watching *The Muppet Show* every night when Brother was finishing his degree in economics (well, truth be told, Daddy always said that Brother actually majored in Sigma Nu and *minored* in economics, but that's probably not an issue we have to settle today). And when I was gearing up for the end of sixth grade, Sister was getting ready to marry Barry and move to Nashville. Sister and Barry bought their first house, for heaven's sake, before I could even drive.

As I got older, though, the distance between our ages became a little easier to navigate. That process was a gradual one, for sure, but I have a vivid memory of when I started to feel like I had something to contribute to the collective sibling conversation. I was in ninth grade, and Daddy and I had traveled to south Mississippi for a family reunion at a beautiful old country church. That particular reunion was the first time that I really wanted to sit around and listen to the stories (as opposed to, oh, walking around the church fellowship hall and making a point to sample all the cobblers), and about two hours into the afternoon, I sat next to my daddy's aunt Cecil at a picnic table. Aunt Cecil had long enjoyed a reputation as a "character" in our family, but since I'd never really experienced the force of her personality live and in person, I figured I'd have a seat next to her and see what all the fuss was about.

I kid you not—I'd been listening to Aunt Cecil's conversation for all of five minutes when I heard her say, "Frankly, I don't know what in the world she wants to have to do with him. I'd rather be alone than have him for a husband. Plus, I've heard for years that when he was in the war he had a run-in with a grenade and got his tallywacker blown off. But that's none of my concern, now is it? If she thinks he'll make a good husband, that's her business, I reckon. SHEWWWWWW."

My favorite part was that when she said the part about the grenade, she reached over and patted me on the arm. LIKE I NEEDED TO MAKE SURE TO SYMPATHIZE.

I may have only been fourteen years old. But I knew the first thing on my Monday morning agenda was to call Sister and Brother and fill them in on the storytelling glory I had just witnessed.

And y'all, it was the strangest thing, but when I told Sister and Brother that story and they laughed out loud, it was like I'd crossed over. Granted, I was still the baby of the family—nothing could ever change that—but I felt like a participant in the conversation instead of just an observer.

And I liked it.

• • •

By the second semester of my freshman year at State, I was fully in the habit of talking to Brother, Sister, and Barry once or twice a week. It was mighty sweet of them to make time for their younger sister like they did;

now that I'm older, I completely recognize that it's no easy feat to include an eighteen-year-old in your life when you're twenty-eight and thirty-two.

And that spring, Sister went above and beyond the call of sibling duty.

Barry's job had taken them from Nashville to his hometown of Atlanta, and in the process of trying to figure out her work situation, Sister reconnected with a friend from college. Over the course of several conversations, Sister and her friend Kerri decided that the timing was perfect for starting their own special events company. Much to their surprise, the new business took off right away (disclaimer: the success of the business shocked absolutely no one else; they were both cute as buttons, smart as whips, and "personality-plus," as my mother-in-law would say), and before the ink had a chance to dry on their new business cards, they'd booked several events for the upcoming summer, which was only a few months away.

So. Faced with an abundance of work and no employees, it dawned on Sister that my cousin Paige and I might enjoy living in Atlanta and working with her and Kerri over our summer break. Paige was finishing her junior year at Ole Miss, and she was as game for a little summertime adventure as I was. The plan was that we'd live at Kerri's house, which is where the business was based, and in addition to all the experience we'd get, we'd earn a little money, too—all while hanging out in the biggest of the Southern cities.

There was absolutely nothing about this plan that didn't appeal to me.

A couple of days after the last exam of my freshman year, I packed my car and drove to Atlanta. Since I felt like it was important to strike the right chord in terms of what was sure to be a very sophisticated summer in the big city, I planned my outfit very carefully. I chose a two-piece maroon ensemble (#HailState) (#GoDogs) with an abstract, cream-colored print all over it, and I paired my stylish knitwear with some fairly horrendous white suede bucks that were my favorite wardrobe item at the time. They reminded me of something Jennifer Grey would have worn in *Dirty Dancing*, and it's only now that it occurs to me that maybe I should have reevaluated my footwear standards.

I also used my fake Ray-Bans as a headband because I thought that made me look cool, like Jami Gertz in *Less Than Zero*.

So I think I've clearly established that I had some questionable style icons.

Hindsight's brutal, y'all.

Since I'd planned most of my road trip sound track well in advance, I made sure that my red canvas cassette tape holder was riding shotgun as I drove east on I-20. I alternated between George Strait, Billy Joel, Amy Grant, the *Dirty Dancing* sound track, and James Taylor, and as I crossed the Georgia state line, I was giddy with independent feelings. I was going to be a CAREER GIRL (well, kind of) and TAKE ATLANTA BY STORM (well, not really) and SET THE CITY ON FIRE (well, not at all, and besides, Atlanta had already been on fire once before, thanks to General Sherman, so obviously my choice of metaphor was dicey at best). If Kelly Clarkson and Destiny's Child had been around back then, I would have been blasting "Miss Independent" and "Survivor" out of my sweet Delco stereo speakers. I might have even rolled down the windows and screamed the lyrics at the Georgia pines, but the Buick's windows weren't always cooperative about rolling back up, and it would have been a shame to let the wind ruin my cool Jami Gertz hair or, even worse, lose those Ray-Ban knockoffs that were worth fives of dollars.

(Also, I feel like I need to point out that even though the Destiny's Child song would have totally fit my mood, I hadn't really survived anything at that point in my life.)

(Well, that's not entirely true.)

(I'd survived the whole acid-washed jeans craze.)

(But that hardly merits a heartfelt rendition of a not-yet-existent pop anthem.)

It was late in the afternoon when I finally arrived in Atlanta, and to my delight, Sister was at Kerri's house when I pulled in the driveway. Kerri lived in a gorgeous older neighborhood off Peachtree Road, and she also drove a Volvo, so she was pretty much the yuppiest person I had ever known. After I said my hellos and unloaded my car and visited with Sister and Kerri in the dining room/makeshift office, I found myself filled with all manner of hope regarding the summer of 1988.

It was going to be awesome.

• • •

Kerri's house was a 1920s bungalow with loads of charm: there were big windows, hardwood floors, and even a few original light fixtures scattered throughout. However, Kerri's husband, who fancied himself a bit of a DIY-er, had passed away unexpectedly several years before, and several of the projects he'd started were still incomplete when Paige and I moved in. We were just young enough to see the unfinished stuff as interesting and not annoying, so we thought it was quirky and fun that the hallway between the kitchen and the dining room didn't actually go anywhere. It was like someone had plopped down a giant, hollow Jenga stick in the most central part of the house, and while it would have made a lovely hallway if it had actually, you know, led to some rooms, as it stood, it gave Kerri some extra storage space for her winter clothes.

The area on the other side of the kitchen was just as perplexing. Kerri's late husband had added on an area that would have eventually been their master bedroom, but again, he'd never completed the project. The room was large enough for Paige and me to share, so it became our sleeping quarters for the summer, but since the final wall and doorway hadn't been finished, the "master" was wide open to the kitchen and the adjacent sunporch, which served as Sister's office. The floor in all three rooms was Spanish tile, and while I can see how that detail might seem unimportant, I just want to emphasize that Paige and I slept in that part of the house, and NOISE.

There are train stations in major metropolitan areas that are more peaceful.

Paige and I didn't care so much, though. We had a couple of twin bed frames—on rollers, no less—and if we got in or out of our beds too quickly, those metal frames would screech across the tile floor and set our teeth on edge, so naturally we'd laugh until we cried. If Kerri decided at two in the morning that she needed a big glass of ice water, we'd wake up to the sounds of her emptying the ice tray and turning on the faucet. Then we'd laugh until we cried. And when Kerri would wake up at dark o'clock to fix her coffee and round up some breakfast and do whatever young entrepreneurs do in the predawn hours, Paige and I would roll over in our respective twin beds, pray the frames didn't scrape the tile, look at each other over our covers, and laugh until we cried.

It was a good thing that just about everything struck us as funny at that stage of our lives. And also that we didn't have a whole lot of needs when it came to our privacy.

• • •

After our first few days in Atlanta, Paige and I both started to understand the lay of the land in terms of our day-to-day responsibilities. Paige worked mainly as an assistant to Sister; they figured out the details for all the upcoming events and worked to make those things happen. I worked mainly as an assistant to Kerri; we wrote letters and designed brochures to secure new business, and I was also supposed to answer the phone and handle all the word processing stuff.

So by nine o'clock every morning, Paige was typically on the sunporch with Sister, and I was in the office off the living room, making my way through Kerri's to-do list. It was my first experience with "working from home," so to speak, and like any good eighteen-year-old, I took great pleasure in sleeping until 8:55 and then stumbling into the office in my pajamas. It honestly never occurred to me that I might be more effective and efficient if I would, oh, *shower*; I mainly just took great pleasure and pride in knowing that working from Kerri's house afforded Paige and me the opportunity to enjoy employment in a modified version of a "no shoes, no shirt, no problem" environment.

And when I'd answer the day's first calls with "Good morning, thank you for calling McMahon Lee Designs," I got a kick out of knowing that the caller had absolutely no idea the Mississippi drawl on the other end of the phone was probably wearing either a Mickey Mouse hospital-style nightgown or a bright-yellow T-shirt dress that had been embellished with puff paint.

I believe the word that you're looking for is *professional.*

• • •

Paige and I had been in Atlanta about two weeks when several business-related details became crystal clear to us. First of all, Kerri liked everything about being a businesswoman. She liked the suits, she liked the lingo, she liked the travel. She dreamed big, talked big, and treated me like a full-fledged assistant. I found this last development all sorts of remarkable, considering I favored pajamas as my preferred work attire.

The second thing we learned was that Sister is the kind of boss everybody wants. She's just the right mix of efficient, fun, and driven—and I'd say that even if we weren't siblings. She and Paige had an absolute blast figuring out the details of different events, building props, contacting vendors, ordering decorations, and planning menus. They're both strangely detail oriented for creative people, and even at eighteen, I marveled at how much *fun* they had figuring out how to bring the vision for a particular party to life. This was quite the epiphany for me considering I've always viewed details as my sworn enemy.

The third thing we learned was that I am not a person who enjoys the business world.

If you'll just go back and reread the first paragraph in this little section, you'll be able to more fully appreciate my dilemma.

I mean, there I was. Eighteen years old. Living rent free in a charming, fun house in the center of Atlanta. I liked answering the phone and working on the computer because, well, I've always enjoyed buttons, but every morning, when Kerri would sit down with me and go over the plan for the day—using words like *strategy* and *return on investment* and *collateral* and *marketing plan*—I'd find myself zoning out and singing Rick Astley lyrics in my head. There was even one day when Kerri set up a meeting between the accountant and me—so the accountant could tell me which bookkeeping tasks I'd be responsible for doing—and about ten minutes into the meeting, I had to excuse myself so I could go to the bathroom and cry. I didn't want to be a baby at all; in fact, I was usually stubborn enough to pretend like I knew what was going on (especially when I didn't) and then figure it out later. But being responsible for even a tiny bit of bookkeeping was so far outside my natural skill set that all I could feel was overwhelmed.

After all, as a wise philosopher once said, "Math ruins everything."

I totally made that up, by the way. And it's probably true only if you're an English major.

But guess what? I was an English major.

So there.

• • •

Not too long after the meeting with the accountant, Sister and Barry invited Paige and me out for Friday-night dinner at a local Mexican place called El Toro.

(I'm certainly not trying to brag, but I happen to know that *el toro* means "the bull.")

(Also, *queso* means "cheese.")

(Be sure to see me for all your translation needs.)

We'd been plowing through the chips and salsa for only a couple of minutes when Barry—who is so kind and genuine and considerate—said, "So. How's everything going at work?"

And oh, bless his heart. He had no idea that he was going to get to play therapist for the rest of the night. An accountant by trade, Barry not only likes numbers, he's also really good with them. So when I tried to explain my frustrations with the NUMBERS and the SALES and the FIGURES—and when I told him I knew beyond a shadow of a doubt that I was not cut out for the business world, he asked what might make the situation better.

"Well," I replied, as I dug into my bean nachos, "I've thought about it a lot, and it seems like the very best thing would be if I just went home."

That wasn't the answer Barry expected.

"*Mississippi* home?" he asked.

"Oh, yeah. ALL THE WAY to Mississippi home."

Sister looked surprised, but she didn't say much. I knew she wouldn't try to persuade me to stay if I was really that miserable, but I also knew that she wouldn't want to see me go.

After supper that night I went back to Kerri's house and wrote Mama and Daddy a long, heartfelt letter. I don't remember my exact words, but I do know that my final sentence was something along these lines: "All this 'real world' stuff is a lot harder than I imagined, and it is stressing me out."

We'll ignore the fact that I was working for a company owned in part by my sister, so TOUGHEN UP, SHIRLEY. And we'll also ignore the part about how I wasn't having to pay any rent or utilities or insurance.

But still. I was having to deal with a LOT of numbers, y'all.

My life was very difficult.

• • •

Considering that I grew up in a town that was less than an hour's drive from a bevy of aunts, uncles, and cousins, spending time with family was never a choice for me. It was just my reality. It was of little to no consequence if I actually *liked* being with them, and now that I think about it, I can't recall a single instance when Mama or Daddy asked my opinion about whether or not I wanted to hang out with relatives on a Sunday afternoon. It was just what we did—like it or lump it—and throughout our childhoods, Paige and I found ourselves in situation after situation where we had to entertain ourselves and make the best of it, regardless of how much we enjoyed the great-aunt we happened to be visiting that day.

Paige and I were born two and a half years apart, and even though that feels like a blip on the age radar now that we're both in our forties, we might as well have been decades apart when we were little. Even still, countless sleepovers and family functions and church services had taught us that we could laugh our way through just about anything; we learned early on that age is practically irrelevant when it comes to matters of the funny bone.

Our history of laughing at, well, *everything* ended up serving Paige and me mighty well in Atlanta. In fact, a big part of why I decided to stay in Atlanta and not hightail it back to Mississippi was that the prospect of spending the rest of the summer with Paige and Sister was too good to pass up. Not even bank statements and THE MANY NUMBERS could deter me. Plus, Kerri had a lot of travel lined up in June, and she told me that I could drive her Volvo while she was out of town, so SOLD.

Kerri's work trips always seemed to usher in some sort of craziness at the house. The first time she left, Paige and I had our first encounter with Kerri's housekeeper, Georgie, who worked every other Monday morning. Georgie was a precious, servant-hearted woman who never missed an opportunity to share an encouraging word. When she'd see me typing on the computer, she'd say, "Well, you sure are mighty smart on that machine, aren't you?" It was several weeks later when I realized that Georgie thought I was *programming* the computer instead of just typing documents, but I appreciated her sweet words nonetheless. When she'd see Paige building a backdrop for an upcoming event, she'd pause and say, "Well, I'll be dog-gone if you aren't the hardest worker there ever was."

Since she typically arrived at Kerri's house early in the morning, Georgie liked to bring her breakfast with her and eat as she worked. Paige and I noticed that Georgie was like our Papaw Davis in that some of her favorite breakfast fare included delicacies like Vienna sausage, potted meat, and plenty of hot sauce to accompany her toast and scrambled eggs. In some parts of the South, that's what's known as a good country breakfast. However, that good country breakfast was not exactly compatible with Georgie's digestive system.

And around nine in the morning, when I'd see Paige's shoulders shake as she pulled her shirt over her nose and moved to another room, I'd know that those Vienna sausages had started to exact their revenge. Paige and I would spend the next couple of hours giving each other nonverbal cues when it was time to CLEAR THE ROOM—sometimes going so far as to open a door or a window under the guise of letting in a little fresh air. We wouldn't have offended Georgie for anything in the world—she was so warm and loving and welcoming to us—but there was no changing the fact that between nine and ten in the morning, she'd consistently leave a mighty stout cloud in her wake. So we tried to handle the situation as best we knew how. Short of offering Georgie some Gas-X, of course.

And since we didn't feel like we knew her well enough to offer remedies for her, you know, *situation*, we held tight to family tradition and let the laughter get us on through.

Let the laughter get us on through.

I'm totally going to cross-stitch that somewhere.

• • •

Since event planning was the whole purpose of Sister and Kerri's company, we spent more than our fair share of nights at corporate dinners and receptions and other business tomfoolery. It's probably no secret that I preferred nights at home with some El Toro takeout and a rerun of *Moonlighting*, but since Kerri was on the road a lot, Sister, Paige, and I became a pretty good setup and takedown crew. It seemed like most of the groups that hired Sister and Kerri wanted to host at least one Southern-themed night during their convention or general meeting or whatever they were having, so Sister and Paige would run by the wholesale florist, purchase what amounted to a van full of flowers, and then artfully display their arrangements in the middle of as many plantation shutters and ferns and stately columns as one conference room could bear.

I've never been much for floral design, so I earned my keep by hauling around boxes and props. While Sister and Paige worked their magic, a caterer would make sure there were plenty of hors d'oeuvres and drinks on hand—preferably some combination involving boiled shrimp, fried catfish, and mint juleps. I personally have lived in the South my whole life without ever sampling a mint julep, but visitors seem to feel it's a rite of passage in these parts. When in Rome, I reckon.

After several weeks, all those smaller parties started to feel pretty routine—almost like a series of dress rehearsals for a big event that was coming up at the end of the summer. A pharmaceutical company was hosting a party for several hundred people at Waverly Hill, a horse farm right outside of town, and it was going to be an all-hands-on-deck event. Sister and Kerri had both worked tirelessly for a couple of months in hopes that everything would go off without a hitch, and Paige and I each had a checklist of what we needed to do before the big night. I may have even kept my checklist in my Day-Timer just so I'd look official and business-y when I picked up chicken biscuits from Mrs. Winner's in Kerri's Volvo.

It didn't matter where I lived, y'all. I was eighteen, and I was forever determined to hunt down the very best fried chicken option and embrace it with my whole heart.

About ten days before the Waverly Hill extravaganza, Kerri had to fly out of town for some meetings. She'd taken the aforementioned Volvo (aka My Baby) to the dealership for service, and she realized about three hours before her flight left that she really needed to take her own car to the airport. If I could remember the reasons for all this, I would tell you, but all I can recall was that there was a lot of urgency and scrambling and a series of events that resulted in my handing her my keys.

So the plan was that Kerri would drive my Buick Regal to the Volvo dealership, leave my keys under the driver's seat mat (Dear Atlanta, you were much more trustworthy back in 1988. Love, Me.), pick up her car, and head to the airport. Then, after work, Sister and Paige—who had been running errands all over town for most of the day—would drive me out to the Volvo place, where I would retrieve the Regal and drive it back to Kerri's house.

Well.

When we got to the dealership, we couldn't find my car anywhere. Kerri said she'd left it in front of the main office, but there was no maroon Buick with Mississippi plates within our line of sight. We figured Kerri must have forgotten some critical detail since she was in such a rush to get to the airport, so I told Sister and Paige that I'd run inside and ask the man at the front desk if he knew anything about it.

The man at the front desk had no knowledge of my car at all, so he called some people and paged some people and talked to some people, and after about five minutes, he called me up to the desk. He had a huge smile on his face, so I figured the news must be good.

"Well, young lady, we've located your car," he said.

"OH, GOOD!" I replied—no doubt with my best sorority girl enthusiasm. "Where is it?"

"At the impound lot," he answered.

"At the what?" I asked, incredulous.

"At the impound lot. It was parked in a loading zone, so we had it towed. Sorry 'bout that. But you'll need to hurry if you want to get it tonight; the lot closes in about twenty minutes, and it's a good ways up the road."

At that point in my life I was unfamiliar with the whole concept of an impound lot. Come to think of it, I don't believe I've had any experience with an impound lot since that sweltering summer day in Fulton County, Georgia. But oh, did I ever get an education within the next half hour.

For example, I learned that impound lots don't care if it's not your fault that your boss left your car in a loading zone.

I also learned that impound lots don't accept out-of-state checks from eighteen-year-olds.

Who knows? Maybe the majority of college freshmen enjoy heftier bank accounts than I did back in the day. But it was going to be almost $200 to get my car out of the lot, and at that stage of my life, that was an amount that I liked to refer to as ALL MY MONEY FOR THE MONTH.

Thankfully Sister and Barry covered my expenses at the impound lot, and of course Kerri repaid them. (She was mortified but utterly tickled when I called her later that night and said, "KERRI. THEY TOWED MY CAR" with all the heartfelt angst of Molly Ringwald in the prom scene of a John Hughes movie.) Sister and Paige didn't stop laughing for about four days.

Once my car was back in my possession, the pre–Waverly Hill preparations should have been easy breezy from that point forward. Paige and I were so confident, in fact, that we decided to pull the phone outside one day and do our work beside Kerri's pool. Sister was meeting with vendors and Kerri was still out of town, so we had more flexibility than we normally enjoyed during a workday.

Really, it wasn't that crazy of an idea if you think about it. These days, people work from all sorts of random locations. Cell phones enable folks to conference call or FaceTime from coffee shops, for heaven's sake. So pulling a two-line business phone to the edge of a patio couldn't have been a big deal, right?

Honestly, it's almost like we were ahead of our time.

• • •

Kerri's pool was another project that her late husband never finished. They installed a pool and a beautiful flagstone patio in the back of the house, but some of the trim work and landscaping features were still missing. When Paige and I first arrived in Atlanta, the water was such a distinct shade of green that you couldn't have paid either of us to stick our toes in the shallow end. You could just barely see the bottom of the pool, and it made me shudder just to think about what might live in that thar cement pond, as Elly May Clampett might say.

Over the course of the summer, though, Kerri had hired a pool service. There was a gorgeous view of the pool area from every room on the back of the house, and it seemed like a good idea to let someone get the pool situation under control before major repairs were required. After three or four visits, the pool service had the pool in tip-top shape, and the day Paige and I planned to work outside was going to be our inaugural dip in those waters, so to speak.

Somehow Paige and I had both managed to make a temporary move to Atlanta without packing swimsuits, and as you might imagine, this wardrobe deficiency presented a challenge for two girls who planned to work by the pool for most of the day. Eventually we decided there was nothing scandalous about sitting poolside in our underwear (keep in mind that this was during a decade when people still loved them some cotton, and a thong was nothing more than a type of sandal people liked to wear in the summertime). So Paige and I and our modest underpinnings took the work party outside, where we prayed to the good Lord that there wasn't a single neighbor with a view of Kerri's backyard.

(Of course we didn't have any sunscreen because we were college students and historically inconsistent with life's daily responsibilities like, for example, SKIN CANCER PREVENTION.)

(Clearly the Bora-Bora lesson had not stuck.)

Nonetheless, the first part of the morning ambled along quite pleasantly. We very deliberately didn't do any splashing when the phone rang (we might have been missing the sunblock, but at least we had the good sense to know that nothing ruins a business call faster than someone screaming "CANNONBALL!"), and even though the pool had been decidedly *ick* just weeks before, its makeover had elevated it to "tranquil oasis" status. Paige and I were just as thrilled as we could be.

A couple of hours into our poolside diversion, I was floating on my back in the center of the pool (to my credit, I was listening for the phone and writing some letters IN MY HEAD) when Paige's voice broke the silence.

"Peach?"

The fact that she invoked my family nickname got my attention.

"PEACH?"

I sat up.

"Don't panic, but, um . . ."

"WHAT IS IT?"

"Well, it's just that you shouldn't get any water in your mouth and you surely don't need to breathe underwater because there's, um, well—there's a dead squirrel floating at the other end of the pool."

"THERE'S A DEAD WHAT FLOATING WHERE?"

Let me tell you that Paige was not kidding.

And listen. I am not by nature what anyone would call a fast-moving individual, but I would venture a guess that my cotton undergarments and I made it out of that pool in four seconds flat. GIDDY ON UP.

We're still not sure where the squirrel came from, by the way. Maybe he'd been lodged in a drain. Maybe he fell from a tree. Maybe it was so hot that he drowned himself when we weren't looking. But since SWIMMING WITH RODENTS was nowhere on my bucket list, it seemed safe to make the call that pool time was over. Granted, working inside at a desk wasn't quite as refreshing, but at least we wouldn't run the risk of contracting some sort of squirrel-transmitted plague.

And to add insult to injury? I got me a mighty fine sunburn that day. It was mainly my chest and shoulders since my legs were in the water most of the time, but it would be several more days before I could convince myself to wear a bra. Plus, since I had been wearing a bra in the pool, my sunburn was particularly noticeable in the places where there had been a lace overlay. I'll leave that to your imagination, but suffice it to say there was a certain Vanity Fair design that I could not ever bring myself to wear again, what with that time I inadvertently let the sun tattoo it to my chest area and all.

• • •

I was still pretty tender skinned when the Friday of the big Waverly Hill party rolled around. Unfortunately, no one had a spare second to care. Sister and Kerri, who obviously was back in town by then, were in charge of details on top of details on top of details, and despite the fact that my personality prefers to get a glimpse of a big picture and then KEEP MOVIN', EVERYBODY, I knew that Paige and I were going to have to hunker down and get after it before the party started at six. We had a U-Haul full of stuff that needed to be unloaded—table linens, gift bags, kids' favors, bottled waters, votive candles, citronella torches, and no small quantity of tree lights—and it took the four of us, Barry, a few of Kerri's friends, and an array of vendors the better part of the day to get everything unpacked and set up.

Guests started to arrive around five thirty, and despite the fact that Paige, Sister, and I looked like Melanie Griffith in *Working Girl* when the steam from the dim sum cart has made her face shiny and her hair frizzy, the setting was magical. Kids jumped in bouncy castles, grown-ups sipped drinks under the oak trees, and the sun was just starting to set on the far side of the property. There was no escaping the scent of citronella, but it only served to make the night seem even more Southern. Considering how our week had started, it was hard to believe that everything had come together—but it did.

The fact that my frizzy hair and sweat-soaked shirt didn't scare any small children when Paige and I were manning the face-painting booth was just an extra measure of blessing. My hunch was that they were at least a little distracted by the man who was making balloon animals. God love him, he was sweating to the point that he had to have been dealing with some dehydration issues. Paige and I looked like Scarlett O'Hara in the shade by comparison.

I'm not trying to be petty about it. But we'd been outside on a July day in Georgia for the better part of sixteen hours. Sometimes you have to find a little comfort where you can.

• • •

Waverly Hill was a working horse farm, so there was a real-live family that lived in the Greek Revival–style home on the property. The owner, a man named Mr. Anderson, could have just as easily been the patriarch in a Tennessee Williams play. The combination of his silver hair, a stature that testified to his love for good food and good liquor, and the omnipresent cigar in his mouth always made me feel like his name should have been "Big Daddy." He called everybody "sugar," "dahlin'," or "good man," and it only took about five minutes in his presence to figure out that he had a flair for the eccentric.

It was after eleven when the last guest drove away from the party, and the McMahon Lee Designs crew was exhausted. Since the U-Haul had to be returned the next day, we were loading it as quickly as we could, and I was in the middle of handing a box to Paige when I heard Mr. Anderson's bourbon-soaked drawl behind me.

"Well, sugar—did everything go okay tonight?"

Paige and I turned around at the same time and were equally bewildered by the sight before us. Mr. Anderson was sporting a driving cap, smoking a cigar, and wearing nothing but a V-neck undershirt and boxers.

I don't know that we've ever worked harder to maintain direct, uninterrupted eye contact in our lives.

We even answered in unison: "Oh, yes, sir! It was great!"

However, what we wanted to say was, "Everything has been fantastic up until this point, but honestly, you've sort of put a damper on things, considering that YOU'RE NOT WEARING PANTS, SIR."

Mr. Anderson seemed not one bit fazed by his attire. He just puffed his cigar, turned the other direction, and walked the expanse of his property like a pants-less king.

• • •

The next day Paige went to visit her then-boyfriend.

(This is an epic tale in and of itself, and I don't have time to tell it.)

(But just know that my personal favorite moment in their relationship was when we were going to Mississippi one weekend, and Boyfriend wouldn't leave the electric locks on Paige's car alone. So she pulled off the interstate, put the car in park, turned to face him, and said, "If you click those locks one more time, you are going to have to figure out a way to walk to Mississippi.")

(And then she eased back onto the road, turned up the radio, and started to sing.)

(It was fantastic.)

Anyway, Paige was with Boyfriend, so Sister, Barry, and I spent the morning running some post-party errands. We were that kind of tired where everything is either utterly hysterical or utterly annoying, and truth be told, we were mostly landing on the "annoying" side of the equation. It was one of those summer days where even the trees seemed hot, and all three of us were ready to wrap up the errands, grab some lunch at El Toro, and then sleep for four or ten hours, preferably underneath the chill of a window unit that had been cranked down to "frigid." But finally—mercifully—we only had one more thing on the must-do list: return the U-Haul that Sister had driven to Waverly Hill.

Since the U-Haul place was just a few minutes down the road—and since we'd left Sister's car there the day before—she asked Barry to go ahead and get a table at El Toro while we returned the U-Haul. We figured it wouldn't take more than fifteen minutes to get everything taken care of, so after we checked the back of the U-Haul to make sure the truck was empty and the dolly that we'd rented was still there, we shut the door and climbed in the cab. Sister was driving; I was mainly there to provide navigational support and perhaps some mild comic relief.

Sister didn't want to have to drive in reverse on any part of the narrow residential streets in Kerri's neighborhood, so we took a slightly round-about route up to Peachtree Road, where Sister managed to make a tight left turn without incident. We slowly moved past all the places that had become so familiar to me over the course of the summer: Turtle's Records, where I'd purchased way too many cassette singles; Oxford Books, where I'd discovered the writing wonder that is Anne Rivers Siddons; El Toro, where at least once a week I commiserated with Sister, Barry, and Paige; and Pier 1, where I'd walked the aisles and wondered if I'd ever be cool enough to own a futon.

Dreams are pretty simple when you're eighteen, aren't they?

Sister was doing her best to stay in the far right lane on Peachtree, which was no small feat, considering the size of that U-Haul and the cramped lanes on a busy stretch of road. We eventually came to a stop at a red light on a hill just past the Pier 1, and I was about to share my Meaningful

Summer Memories with Sister when we heard a sound from the back of the truck that was most definitely an explosion.

Okay. So it wasn't really an explosion. But I'll be doggone if it didn't sound like one. Sister and I stared at each other for a split second, neither of us having any earthly idea what had happened, and just as I was getting ready to ask Sister if maybe someone had hit us from behind, I looked in the side mirror and realized that we must not have fastened the back door as securely as we thought we had.

Because that dolly we'd rented from the U-Haul folks was sliding down Peachtree Road faster than a redneck driving in an ice storm on bald tires.

Sister threw the U-Haul into park, and we both jumped out. We were like Jill and Kris Munroe on *Charlie's Angels*—except we were chasing a dolly instead of, you know, an evil hypnotist or the head of an underground gambling ring. And also we weren't private detectives and had never to my knowledge driven Mustangs. Even still, I remember thinking very clearly that there was no way we were going to catch that dolly unless a car or a curb got in its way.

Or maybe Sabrina Duncan could come to our rescue. She always seemed to run superfast, whereas Kelly Garrett seemed much more concerned about her hair.

Fortunately—mercifully—the dolly took a turn and ran into the curb. Sister and I managed to corral it and wheel it back to the truck, where we hoisted it into the back and made sure the lock was fully fastened and secure this time. The oddity of the whole experience was lost on us until the second Sister turned the lock—and then we started to laugh so hard we couldn't breathe. I don't think either one of us made a sound as our mouths hung open and the tears ran down our faces; we were so stooped over from hysterics that it was a battle to even walk back to the cab of the truck. I finally had to stop and will myself to stand up straight, and when I did, I added one more Peachtree Road memory to my personal collection.

I'd bought music there. I'd read books there. I'd window-shopped for furniture there. And thanks to the rogue dolly that escaped the confines of our U-Haul, I'd also wet my pants there.

Amen and amen.

• • •

Just between us, I was kind of a hot mess when I was eighteen. Oh, I was sweet enough and nice enough and knew how to play the good little church girl as well as anybody. I kept my public rebellion to a minimum because I didn't want anybody to talk about me, but I was way more interested in a good reputation than a transformed heart (this is a pattern that I would not lay down for several more years). And I certainly didn't have enough sense to "invest" in my family relationships—because as far as I was concerned, the world sort of revolved around me. I went to Atlanta for purely selfish reasons: I thought it would be a whole lot more fun than spending the summer in my hometown. It never occurred to me that it would be a great opportunity to spend time with my relatives. Even after I got there and the "fun" part started to seem less likely, I just figured that, worst-case scenario, I was going to spend the summer balancing bank statements and talking to clients and figuring out all the features of WordPerfect.

And I did do those things.

But I also learned lessons I never expected. For one thing, I learned that Paige, Sister, and I share way more than a bloodline. I learned that, oddly enough, all three of us are people who are willing to literally walk on each other's backs to guarantee a good "pop" (maybe that's why I'm typing this twenty-six years later and wondering what that nagging pain in my neck might be). I learned that even if you graduated from high school more than a decade apart, Boz Scaggs and James Taylor will always provide some musical common ground. I learned that a whole host of life's problems can be solved with chips, cheese dip, and people who love you sitting around the table.

And I learned that even if Sister and Paige weren't related to me, I'd still think that they were two of the most kind, creative, hilarious people I'd ever known.

Because when I got to Atlanta, they were my family.

But when I left Atlanta, they were my friends.

I'd call that a win.

CHAPTER 8

WHEN A DISCIPLE OF THE LORD DRIVES A GRAY HONDA ACCORD

AT THE BEGINNING of my sophomore year at State, I would have told you that I was full to the brim in the friends department. I'd found my tribe, so to speak, and one of the people in that tribe was Daphne, a beautiful, hilarious, athletic girl from Starkville whose skin and hair were a point of borderline obsession for my mama. In fact, I couldn't even mention Daph's name without Mama saying, "Oh, Sophie. I do know that she has THE MOST GORGEOUS skin and hair I have ever seen. She is just STUNNING." Mama was right. She was also thrilled when I told her that Daph and I had decided to room together our sophomore year, and I think she secretly hoped that living with Daphne might reinforce Mama's lifelong instruction to take off my makeup every night before I went to bed and maybe even to exfoliate regularly.

Daph and I lived on the south side of campus in a huge dorm that we wholeheartedly believe is responsible for at least 95 percent of the sinus infections we've enjoyed since we left it. Mold spores aside, though, living with Daph meant that I spent a good part of every night alternating between hysterical laughter and deep, philosophical conversations that made my head hurt (this is still my preferred structure to daily life, by the way). When Daph wasn't around, I'd devote thirty or forty-five minutes to playing Whitney Houston's "One Moment in Time" over and over at an annoyingly high volume, and inevitably I'd walk down the hall to find some company. My Myrtlewood friend Marion and her roommate, Wendi, were two doors down, and their room was always an excellent home base before we'd make our afternoon rounds. Having so many good friends on the same hall ensured that there was always somebody to talk to, and even though my classes were more demanding and my schedule was less wide open than it was during my freshman year, I thrived on that near-constant social interaction.

(This was a few years before my inner introvert very timidly raised her hand and then politely asked if we could please figure out a way to find a little more quiet in the day-to-day.)

(As long as everybody else felt like it was a good idea.)

(And if it wouldn't inconvenience anyone, of course.)

So for that first half of my sophomore year, the recurring theme or motif or whatever you want to call it was ALL THE PEOPLE. We went out to dinner, we took road trips (including one particularly memorable one when Daph and I listened to the Doobie Brothers all the way to New Orleans and back, but I will not share the details of that trip at this juncture since I have a son who can in fact read and I would prefer not to be a stumbling block on his personal path to godly behavior and also holiness), we cheered at football games, we visited each other's hometowns, we hung out in our dorm rooms, we sang together in our cars, we spied on crushes, and we raided the giant Magic Markers in the Chi O house so we could make each other door signs for birthdays or big dates.

A big ole pile-o-relational-fun is what it was.

But what I couldn't seem to figure out—wonder though I did—was how to incorporate all the "walking with Jesus" business into my life at college. Oh, I gave it mighty good lip service and might have even cracked open my Bible a time or three, but to put it in Southern Baptist terms: I was strugglin'. I don't know that anyone had me on a prayer list or anything like that, but I was standing on the edge of the wilderness.

And something about that wide-open wilderness—even though I knew it was vast and endless and lonely—was strangely appealing to me.

• • •

Late October was when the Chi Os usually held officer elections for the next calendar year. And listen. I know that for lots of folks the whole sorority/fraternity thing isn't worth much more than an eye roll. I get it. In fact, now that I'm a mama, I have approximately zero desire for Alex Hudson to join a fraternity when he gets to college. That being said, my own experience with sorority life was pretty idyllic, and my memories are happy ones. I'm glad we had this talk.

So when elections rolled around the fall of my sophomore year, I didn't really have any burning desire to take on a pressure-packed leadership position. Come to think of it, I've *rarely* had a desire to take on a pressure-packed leadership position. I love to be involved with different organizations and causes, but my preferred place for doing that is at a considerable distance from any sort of spotlight and/or attention. Perhaps this is why, when I was in seventh grade and had my first opportunity to run for a student government office, I looked at all the options and thought, *Well, assistant secretary seems like it will be just my speed.*

In fact, I'll never forget the night I asked my daddy to sign the permission slip so I could run.

"I think it's great that you're running," he said. "But don't you want to aim a little higher? Maybe take on a little more responsibility?"

"No, sir," I replied. "I think I'm good. This will be perfect."

It was maximum involvement with minimum risk, a pattern that I'm sort of ashamed to tell you has held steady for the better part of thirty years. Keep in mind that from the time I was sixteen until I was about twenty-eight, there was nothing that seemed more appealing to me than working as a background singer for James Taylor. To my way of thinking, it was the perfect job: not too mainstream, not too trendy—but a loyal, established audience that makes for a safe performance environment.

(The fact that I had next to no talent in terms of singing was never a consideration.)

(I felt certain that we'd work out all of those pretend details for my pretend job at my pretend audition.)

Well.

When that year's Chi O officer elections were over, I was the new corresponding secretary, a role that couldn't have been more perfect for my behind-the-scenes-please personality. The corresponding secretary had two primary responsibilities—checking the mail and writing thank-you notes—and since I could do both of those things in my sweats and/or pajamas, I felt like the required skills were well within my personal wheelhouse. I may not be good at much, people, but I can for sure unlock a post office box and write some sentences thanking a bunch of fraternity boys for, like, THE BEST SWAP EVER. I was perfectly comfortable with my ability to fulfill my duties.

However, there was one part of being an officer that gave me pause: I was going to have to move into the sorority house, which meant I was going to have to leave my beloved Daph. Granted, I'm sure Daph and I did things to get on each other's nerves when we lived together, but we were both night owls, we were both overthinkers, and we were both far too familiar with all the John Hughes movies. That was all we needed.

Since there was only one other sophomore officer—a blonde, green-eyed girl from Alabama who was the new pledge trainer—I suspected we'd be roommates when we moved into the house in January. And keep in mind: I wasn't looking for any new close friends. Emma Kate and I actually lived across the hall from each other in the dorm, but we'd never really run in the same circles. In addition to being a very busy marketing major, Emma Kate was superinvolved in a couple of campus ministries (which I was, um, NOT), so she liked to "wake up early" and "get dressed for the day" and "schedule her time." This level of discipline didn't necessarily line up with my personal approach to college life, which was more along the lines of "HEY! I know I have a botany test at eight tomorrow morning, but if we go to the Randy Travis concert and stop by Allgood's for cheeseburgers after and then ride around and sing old Steve Miller Band songs until about two in the morning, I can still study for FIVE HOURS before I take a quick shower and go to class!"

I am not saying that my methods were successful. I am simply saying that they were my methods.

And I am also saying that I was somewhat delusional.

• • •

Even though Emma Kate and I had never hung out very much, we certainly weren't strangers. We'd visited off and on throughout that fall semester and started to get to know each other when I knocked on her door after I realized that I'd been hearing the same Amy Grant song playing on the other side of her door for the better part of two weeks. As it turned out, Emma Kate had been asked to sing a solo at the next Fellowship of Christian Athletes meeting, so she'd been practicing "In a Little While" like crazy. I thought she had to be about ninety-four varieties of brave since she'd agreed to sing in front of other people, but Emma Kate, who tackles every challenge in her life head-on, wasn't fazed in the least.

One afternoon I even sat in EK's dorm room and listened to her practice her song a couple of times—a process that just fascinated me to no end because, as a general rule, I never like to rehearse anything in front of anybody because I am far too self-conscious. Emma Kate, on the other hand, has always valued feedback and constructive criticism, and EVEN NOW I CANNOT BEGIN TO TELL YOU HOW UNCOMFORTABLE THIS LEVEL OF VULNERABILITY MAKES ME.

Please pardon me for one moment while I take some deep breaths and lo, perhaps even a dab of anti-anxiety medication.

I told Emma Kate that I thought her song was real pretty, and after she talked for a minute or so about whether she needed to sing a certain part higher or lower, she said, "Hey! Why don't you go *with* me to FCA this week? It'll make it easier for me to sing if there's a friendly face, and besides, you'll get to hear a good message from the speaker!"

And then I think she may have winked.

My affection for sleeping in on Sunday mornings wasn't exactly a big secret.

But that affection had never run up against the persistent evangelism of a sassy little firecracker from Hamilton, Alabama.

• • •

Now this is only my opinion—certainly not some proven theory—but in many cases, I think, moving our faith from the (mostly) safe environments of our home churches and our childhood homes into dorm rooms and first apartments and college literature classes involves a fair amount of spiritual wrestling. Because while I know with everything in me—and the Lord and I have discussed this on countless occasions—that He "began a good work in [me]" (Philippians 1:6) when I was in ninth grade at Camp Wesley Pines, there was a point around seventeen or eighteen when that "good work" was like a boat with a flooded engine.

Seriously. I felt like I was out in the middle of a lake, trying over and over to get the whole faith thing cranked up again. But mostly it was just a lot of noise, a lot of smoke, and a lot of flailing about while I floated around in pretty much the exact same place.

So by my nineteenth birthday, I had more questions than answers. Did I believe in God? Yes. Did I believe that His Son, Jesus, died on the cross as the sacrificial atonement for my sin? Absolutely. Did I believe that part of the Apostles' Creed that I'd faithfully recited for most of my life—the part that says, "The third day he rose from the dead; he ascended into heaven, and sitteth at the right hand of God the Father Almighty; from thence he shall come to judge the quick and the dead"?

Amen.

Yep. Sure did.

Did I have any idea how all that stuff was supposed to inform and impact and illuminate my day-to-day life?

Nope. Sure didn't. And I was too prideful, too stubborn, too ashamed to admit to anyone that while, yes, I was crystal clear on the major points of my salvation, I was pretty foggy on what it meant to really walk out that thing.

So as a result, I did something we're especially good at doing down here in the Bible Belt: I pretended.

I played church.

And I told myself that was enough.

There were all kinds of problems that led to this pattern of going through the spiritual motions, of course—starting with some faulty theology and then working out from there. If I'd read a lick of *The Great Gatsby* at that point of my life, surely to goodness I would have seen bits and pieces of myself in Jay Gatsby and Daisy Buchanan and the myriad ways they created elaborate facades that they wanted to believe were real. Because if I were honest, I'd have admitted that I was much more interested in playing the part of Sweet Christian Girl than I was in seeing the Lord transform my mind and my heart.

And the bottom line, I reckon, is that what I really wanted was for Him to make me look good. I wanted to be a good girl with a good reputation. I wanted to have good friends and get a good degree and find a good job. I looked forward to the time when I'd marry a good man and buy a good house in a good neighborhood and drive a good car and maybe have a couple of good kids who would, naturally, go to good schools.

But God's best? Oh, that was *nowhere* on my spiritual radar.

So in the midst of all that, you might be thinking that my spiritual life was pretty bleak in the year of our Lord 1989.

And you'd be right about that.

But let me tell you what the Lord did.

He sent me a pledge trainer named Emma Kate Payne.

• • •

The night of Emma Kate's big solo at FCA, I decided I might as well tag along. I'd tried going to a couple of different Christian organizations that met on campus at State, but I never made them a priority. Plus, since I was walking around with so many questions, I couldn't shake the feeling that everybody at Reformed University Fellowship or Campus Crusade or wherever was fully trained in Living the Christian Life, and I was the kid sitting in the back of the room who couldn't quite seem to catch on.

And let me be clear: I could have gone to my parents or my high school youth group leader or about a hundred other people at any point and confessed the specifics of my struggle and blurted out my questions and listened to some wise counsel. But I didn't. My pride told me that I shouldn't, and I didn't see any point in arguing.

Emma Kate and I zipped over to the FCA meeting in her gray Honda Accord, and after she parked and retrieved all her audio equipment, we walked to the cafeteria in the athletic dorm. The first order of business after we arrived was to set up Emma Kate's boom box on the podium, and while I realize that today we could set up a theater-class sound system using only an iPhone and a pair of pocket-size speakers, the late eighties were a different technological day.

I didn't know anybody at the meeting besides Emma Kate, so I found a seat and smiled awkwardly while she visited with a few of her football player friends. I contented myself by thinking that I looked pretty cute in my red corduroy skirt and my oversize mock-turtleneck sweater with a giant bar code and "ETC." emblazoned on the front.

After the introductory prayer and a few remarks by somebody I didn't know, Emma Kate stood up to sing.

I was off-the-charts nervous for her. But after she finished the first verse, she looked totally at peace as she started to sing the chorus. As someone who'd practically earned a minor in the music of Amy Grant, I'd heard the song hundreds of times. But one part of that chorus jumped out at me:

We're just here to learn to love him
We'll be home in just a little while.

Fair enough, Amy.

But I was increasingly certain that I might need some lessons and maybe even some directions.

• • •

Emma Kate and I were supposed to move into the Chi O house after New Year's, and over Christmas break she called me at my parents' house to talk about important things like matching comforters and throw pillows. We gradually shifted into a discussion about what we'd been doing over Christmas break, so I told her all about my high school friends and the fifty-three ways we'd celebrated Christmas together over the course of about eight days. Any visit to Myrtlewood during my college years tended to be an exercise in community building: we went to the movies, visited with each other's parents, rotated from one house to the next, and traveled up, down, and over narrow rural roads while we sang R.E.M. and George Michael and Robert Palmer. Our time together was effortless, but even then, I think, we knew to treasure it, to hold it tight, to take good care of it. We were nineteen and all too aware that Real Live Adulthood was just around the corner, and golly-dog if our mamas hadn't taught us how to treasure those friendships and love each other really well.

Emma Kate asked lots of questions about our tight-knit group of folks; since she had graduated from a much smaller high school in a much smaller town, she'd had a different experience (not necessarily worse—just different). She told me about several of her close friends, including one who attended a small Christian college. EK went on to relay a story that friend had told her, and while I don't remember all the details, I do know that there was talk of spiritual warfare, demon possession, and maybe even an exorcism.

I'm gonna tell you one subject that had never, to my knowledge, come up for discussion at the Methodist church where I grew up: ANY OF THAT.

No kidding. I didn't even know how to respond. I just remember standing in Mama's kitchen, twisting the phone cord, and saying variations of "Oh, no" over and over.

"Oh, no!"

"OH NO!"

"Ohhhhh. No."

I think that the story had a happy ending—or at least as happy as it could be considering someone had, in fact, battled demons—and I hung up from our conversation with two primary thoughts: (1) I bet Emma Kate won't pretend to be Charlie's Angels like Daph did, and (2) those Baptists are pretty hard core about that spiritual warfare business. I mean, yes, I'd watched EK sing an Amy Grant song at FCA, and I knew that her walk with the Lord was the most important aspect of her life, but part of me wondered if she was going to try to lead me in two-hour devotions every night and then cart me off to revivals on the weekends.

I just wasn't sure how all that was going to fit into my demanding social calendar.

Plus, I'd worked long and hard to keep God at a safe distance, and quite frankly, I wasn't too sure I was ready for a roommate who would more than likely see me as her personal mission field.

• • •

One thing that consistently annoys me about the book of Proverbs is that it just humbles the fire out of me. And in Proverbs 19:21, there's this little nugget-o-wisdom: "Many are the plans in the mind of a man, but it is the purpose of the LORD that will stand."

That verse does not necessarily cooperate with my control-freak tendencies.

But I didn't really know that spiritual truth when I moved into the Chi O house in January of my sophomore year, and as a result, I had very clear ideas about how it would all work out. EK and I would be friends, sure, but I wasn't going to let her or Jesus get too close. I was perfectly content to chart my own course, keep all my questions to myself, and continue to let my Bible serve as a convenient coaster—albeit a dusty one—on the bookshelf above my bed.

The more I watched EK, though, the more I saw that there was something different about her consistency with Jesus. It's not that my other friends weren't believers—because for the most part, all of them were—it's just that there was a depth to EK's walk that stood out to me. She wasn't some goody-goody Pollyanna, and there were definitely areas where she struggled (I will let her tell you about the night a cute boy from BSU invited someone else to his fraternity's formal dance, and EK was so angry that she slammed and even kicked our door so many times that she finally collapsed on the floor of our room while I covered my mouth and tried to remain sympathetic and also not laugh my head off).

But here's what set EK apart, at least in my mind. She believed in doing things with excellence so that God would be glorified. She faithfully spent time in Scripture. She honored her parents with her words and her decisions. She fled temptations. She prayed with expectancy.

And she loved her friends—including me, who didn't have much to offer her except my brokenness and my compromise and my inconsistency—unconditionally.

It was a sermon that preached to me on a deeper level than most of what I'd heard in church.

I just wasn't quite sure how I was supposed to respond.

CHAPTER 9

BY ALL MEANS, LET'S ATTEND
TO THE SUPERFICIAL

THE SUMMER AFTER our sophomore year, I went back to Myrtlewood to babysit, and Emma Kate went to about three different states to work as a counselor at various FCA youth camps (as you do). It was difficult for us to stay in touch because texting and e-mail weren't even invented yet (well, I guess someone had actually invented them, but cell phones were still the size of two bricks stacked on top of each other, and using e-mail would have required us to go to the computer lab at State, so no), and since EK was all over the place, I never really knew the best way to keep up with her. The good news was that there were lots of folks home in Myrtlewood that summer, including Marion, and thanks to a passel of recently graduated friends from State who were getting married that June and July, I knew I'd have ample opportunity to see Tracey, Elise, and Daph at weddings. The summer was full of promise, I tell you.

That summer also marked a pretty significant decision on my part. I'd gained about forty pounds since I started college (please see that earlier chapter about Popeyes, and don't forget to factor in late-night hamburgers, French fries, and cheese sticks), and I kept thinking that if I could get the weight off, then maybe that would temper my increasing confusion. Keep in mind that you'd have never known I felt that way unless we were superclose friends or, like EK, you lived with me. I guess I figured that since I hadn't ironed out all of my faith issues, maybe I'd just tackle my physical ones instead.

(In the interest of transparency, I should tell you that I'm still fighting those stinkin' physical battles even as I'm typing this.)

(Because, yes, while I'm sipping on ice water this afternoon, what I would really prefer is a Caffè Mocha with whole milk and a piece of Starbucks banana-walnut bread.)

(Perhaps I will chronicle this struggle in greater detail in a future book that I have tentatively titled *Bacon Is My BFF—and Other Lies I Tell Myself.*)

(But I digress.)

Liquid diets were all the rage back then, so I signed on to be a part of a program that was offered through my doctor's office—an irony that, in retrospect, makes me a little cringe-y. Sure, I could have chosen to cut back on my portions and exercise daily and make healthier choices, but I wanted some quick results. After all, I'd seen plenty of movies and TV shows where a girl who struggled with her weight looked like a completely new person after she ran in place for six minutes, attempted a few awkward push-ups, put on some mascara, parted her hair on the opposite side, and bought some stylish new clothes.

SIGN ME UP.

And seriously, there's really not world enough or time enough to dig deeply into this particular topic, and I feel a little weird writing about it because it's an area of my life where I just haven't had significant, long-term victory, but none of that changes the fact that when I was nineteen years old, I had some serious weight-loss plans, and I meant business, by diggity.

I didn't waste any time once I got home to Myrtlewood; I started the liquid diet the first week of summer break. I had an initial physical exam and weigh-in with my doctor, and that first weigh-in really cemented my internal sentiment that "IT'S TIME TO PUT DOWN THE FRIED CHICKEN, GLADYS."

So I did. I put down the fried chicken and the fried okra—and the fried dill pickles, too. For the next two months I faithfully mixed my "chocolate" (oh, do I ever use that term loosely) powder with water and choked down supplement shakes three times a day. By the end of the second week I could barely smell that powder without retching—which, in hindsight, was probably a physiological sign that HUMANS ARE NOT MEANT TO INGEST THIS SUBSTANCE—but I pushed through because of my desire to be a Liquid Diet Overachiever. I drank the shakes, I heated the broth, I ate the little cookies made of cardboard and a few underutilized grains that were supposed to qualify as a sweet treat.

Somehow—and this totally confounds me because I was subsisting on a few hundred calories a day—I even mustered up enough energy to exercise. Emma Kate had introduced me to Sandi Patty's music the previous semester, so in the mornings or afternoons I'd pop the *Make His Praise Glorious* cassette in my Walkman and hoof it around Mama and Daddy's front yard, down to the pasture, and back up to the front yard, and then I'd repeat the same route until I felt light headed or overheated, whichever came first.

(I know. It's ridiculous.)

(That's why I'm sitting here thinking back on that time and shaking my head at my own dadgum self.)

When the heat got to be too much, I'd take my workout inside. I really liked to play Sandi's *Songs from the Heart* as the sound track for some light aerobics. And if you've ever heard "Pour on the Power," you totally understand where I'm coming from—because if there was ever a contemporary Christian song that begged for a double-quick crossover step, that one was it.

• • •

It seems like whenever someone I know embarks on a quest to lose weight, that person will usually get to the second or third week of healthier living and start saying, "You know, I'm just not hungry anymore! I don't really have any cravings! I'm totally satisfied by eating a cup of boiled cabbage and then taking a few deep breaths! I even forget to eat sometimes!"

Well, that was not really my experience. There was rarely a time when I didn't want gigantor helpings of asparagus casserole or creamed potatoes or, you know, the entirety of the hot bar at Quincy's (somebody say it with me: "HOMEMADE YEAST ROLLS"). However, I was determined to have my personal made-for-TV movie experience when I went to Starkville; I wanted people to be astounded and amazed and awestruck by the progress I'd made. So I stuck to my guns and stuck to my diet and felt really good about the way the numbers on the scale kept sliding on down.

But in the back of my mind, I think I knew those results were going to be temporary. They *had* to be temporary—because the only way my metabolism was going to cooperate was if I continued to starve myself. And that's exactly what I was doing: starving myself. That realization cemented itself about a month into the summer when my body said, "NO MORE" and I almost fainted in Walmart. The steady rotation of shakes and broth and, lo, even more shakes had left me feeling as weak as a day-old kitten, and my crash diet finally caught up with me somewhere between the outdoor grills and the wicker settees. One minute Mama and I were looking at patio furniture, and the next minute I was breaking into a cold sweat, watching the ceiling fade to black, and collapsing onto a lawn chair.

I believe this is what nutritional experts might call a WARNING SIGN.

I tried to make a joke about it (imagine that), but it scared the fire out of me. I was shaking, I was hungry, and I was more than a little freaked out by how fatigued I was. Fortunately Mama was there to make sure that I was okay, and once I started to feel better and she was satisfied that she didn't need to take me to the doctor's office, she promptly drove me home and cooked me two steaks.

She wouldn't let me out of her sight until I'd eaten every single bite.

Baby girl here was a smidge deficient in protein.

• • •

It was the beginning of August when I loaded my car and drove back to Starkville. I was fortyish pounds lighter than I'd been in May, and I felt a small surge of pride as I buckled my seat belt and pushed James Taylor's *Greatest Hits* into the cassette player. I was on my way to my junior year of college, and everything about the trip felt familiar to me—except for my smaller size. I turned on Highway 45 and drove north, seemingly on auto-pilot, coasting through towns with names like Electric Mills and Scooba and Shuqualak. I was almost to Highway 82—which runs straight into Starkville—when I turned left onto Sessums Road and dodged a litany of potholes for the sake of a "shortcut" back to campus. It never occurred to me that those rural-road potholes didn't really cut off any time from my trip; I'd convinced myself that the supposed shorter route must surely be the better way.

Come to think of it, that's precisely the kind of thinking that will eventually cause a near-fainting spell in the Walmart Lawn and Garden Center after approximately four weeks of a crash diet.

Funny how that works.

Eventually I pulled into my favorite parking space at the Chi O house, and as I lugged my duffel bags and milk crates full of clothes and books and heated hair-curling implements to my new room on the back hall, I contemplated how much different and better my college life was going to be now that I wasn't carrying the burden of all that extra weight. There was just so much to look forward to: I couldn't wait to see EK and hear all about her summer, I couldn't wait to share my personal weight-loss story just like people did on those late-night Richard Simmons commercials, and I couldn't wait to reconnect with my friends and get back in the swing of school and maybe even wear my running tights to rush meetings in case somebody wanted to tell me how good my calves looked and I could pretend like I didn't know what they were talking about even though I'd probably been standing on my tiptoes and flexing for the better part of fifteen minutes.

Subtlety has never really been my gift, I'm sad to say.

Emma Kate rolled into town a couple of days later, and after she put away all her clothes and I stopped drooling over her Eagle's Eye sweater collection from which I planned to borrow early and often, we set out for lunch so she could tell me about everything the Lord had done at her FCA camps. Naturally, I was super excited to tell her about all my newfound self-discipline and how I knew beyond a shadow of a doubt that I wasn't going to gain back the weight, NOT EVER, YES MA'AM, BELIEVE IT.

To Emma Kate's credit, she listened to me very patiently and did not roll her eyes even one time.

In retrospect it's interesting to me that our summers were so opposite. Emma Kate nourished her spirit while I starved my body. She was full to the brim with the goodness of the Lord, and I was so stinkin' hungry that all I could think about was which restaurant might serve some kind of fried-food sampler (a sure sign that my diet was on the verge of imminent destruction). In our own ways, I reckon, Emma Kate and I both had to figure out how to acclimate to Starkville after spending the summer in our respective bubbles. Emma Kate had lived on the spiritual mountaintop for the better part of two months, and while I *thought* I'd been on a wellness mountaintop of my own, I'd really just camped out in a big ole desolate valley.

A valley that was unrealistically devoid of foods that are cooked in peanut oil.

So there we were. I was trying to figure out how to deal with all the food, and Emma Kate was trying to figure out how to deal with, well, all the worldly. To her credit, she seemed determined to pray both of us through our transitions, and it was then—at our first back-to-State lunch—when I became aware that one of Emma Kate's takeaways from her time at the FCA camps was a tendency to whisper pray. I was a little taken aback by it at first, but since EK is anything but a poser (she is, honest to goodness, the most sincere person I know), I decided that the whisper praying was rooted in a deep well of expectancy about what the Lord was going to do after she offered up her thanksgivings and petitions. It occurred to me that she must be whispering so she'd be able to hear the Holy Spirit at any moment, and honestly, I was borderline fascinated by her new level of intimacy with the Lord.

I quickly learned that the whisper praying could get awkward in a group, though. One night several of us were sitting around a table together, about to eat supper, and Emma Kate offered up a lengthy, heartfelt blessing with such hushed fervor that I finally cocked one eye open and looked around the table. When I realized that Elise was looking back at me, I silently mouthed a question that seemed increasingly pressing:

DOES SHE KNOW THAT WE CAN'T HEAR HER?

Elise shrugged and quickly closed her eyes; I suspect she didn't want to be caught with her eyes open when the Holy Spirit inevitably showed up.

I mean, how could He possibly resist all that whispering?

The adjustments on my end of things turned out to be harder than I'd thought. Since I'd spent most of my summer avoiding food—save those steaks Mama made me eat after my sinking spell at Walmart (well, there was also one night when I was so desperate for something crunchy that I drove to the store and bought a bag of Ruffles and a container of French onion dip and pretty much confirmed once and for all that I am drawn to a simple carbohydrate like a moth to flame)—I hadn't really worked out how to *live* with it, which was a way bigger and more important issue. I'd also failed to consider that eating out was a huge part of our social life at college, and what worked for me in Myrtlewood didn't fare so well in Bulldog Country. It seemed like there was temptation at every turn because, well, there was temptation at every turn: fried broccoli bites at Harveys, fried shrimp po'boys at Oby's, fried catfish at the Little Dooey.

Perhaps you're noticing that "fried" was a bit of a theme.

But—just as it can be now—the combination of good food and good company was too much to resist, and before I knew it, I was driving in reverse on my personal weight-loss course.

Seriously. I think I gained eight pounds in four days. In hindsight, Emma Kate's whisper praying seems like a total nonissue compared to how quickly I backed off my original goal of sharing my weight-loss victory and turned into a walking billboard with an ever-present slogan plastered on the front: "FOLLOW ME IF YOU'D LIKE TO FIND THE CHEESE FRIES."

Gradually, though, we settled back into the rhythm of college life, and the days started to follow a predictable pattern: I'd wake up, shower, and amble over to Elise and Tracey's room for some early morning conversation (to be clear, the conversation was usually with Elise; Tracey has always been a gifted sleeper, so I could sit on her bed, blow-dry my hair, sing an operatic rendition of the national anthem, and maybe even light a couple of sticks of dynamite without disturbing Tracey's REM cycle). Then I'd walk down to

Daph's room and analyze an Indigo Girls song or two before I'd get ready for class, drive over to Lee Hall to take care of all my academic business, head back to the house, hang out in Wendi and Marion's room, laugh until suppertime, then find a friend or two and ride around Starkville and sing until we were too tired or hoarse to keep going.

In retrospect, it wasn't exactly a *high-pressure* time of my life.

But oh, my fickle heart. It was just so stinkin' restless.

And the liquid diet, the forty fewer pounds, the smaller-size skirts— well, much to my disappointment, they hadn't done a single thing to change that.

• • •

For as long as I've known her, Emma Kate has been superorganized. She's really good at figuring out what needs to go where and then sticking to her system. I, on the other hand, tend to put things in places that don't make sense. Right now, for example, I have lightbulbs stored above the washing machine and toilet paper next to paintbrushes in a laundry-room basket because SURE, THAT SEEMS LOGICAL, and I am apt to get nineteen kinds of frustrated when I can't find my favorite earrings and then remember, *Oh, wait—I've been keeping all my jewelry in that piece of pottery next to the oven.*

Emma Kate's predictability with what goes where was an odd comfort to me when we lived together. For example, I always knew I could find her spare car key on the right-hand side of her bottom drawer, and she faithfully stacked her sweaters in the most orderly way on the top of the built-in shelves on her side of the room. Her Bible, journal, and devotional book lived on the ledge over the top of her bed; her selection of Christian aerobics videos (because OH, YES, that was totally a thing back then) stayed on the second shelf of our TV stand; and the memory verses she'd written on index cards filled the bottom half of her bulletin board.

Oh, those memory verses—I don't know if Emma Kate had any idea how often I'd stand next to her bed, look at that bulletin board, and try to figure out how those verses applied to my life. Here's the one I remember more than any other:

For to me to live is Christ, and to die is gain.
PHILIPPIANS 1:21

Quite frankly, I just wasn't entirely sure what to make of that.

I mean, I got the sentiment of what Paul was trying to say to the church at Philippi: your true life is in Christ, not in your selfish desires.

But did he really have to take it one step further and say, "To die is gain"? SERIOUSLY, PAUL?

Honestly, that verse annoyed me to no end and flew in the face of everything I wanted to believe about my life. Because to my way of thinking, since it was in fact *my* life, it should be about my wants and my wishes and my comfort and my plans and my happiness. I didn't want to miss out on a single thing that I deemed being worth my energy or my time—no matter how potentially destructive that thing might be—and even though I'd said yes to life in Christ when I was fourteen, I was scared to think about what changes would inevitably come my way if I really and truly embraced my own death.

Does that make sense?

Let me put it this way: I could look at Emma Kate's life and see consistent sacrifice and surrender all over it. I, on the other hand, was the queen of compromise, and I LIKED IT THAT WAY. I liked that I had a little streak of rebellion that reared its head at Nickel Draft Beer Night every now and again. I liked that while I was a "good girl," I wasn't a Goody Two-shoes. I liked that I lived with a foot on each side of the fence, because that meant my faith never made me uncomfortable. I liked that I could change and adapt and chameleon so I fit right in no matter where I was.

But Paul, you see, wasn't having any of that with the church of Philippi—and he wasn't having any of it with me, either. His worldview was crystal clear.

Here's what life is: Christ.

Here's what death is: gain.

Next question?

So every day—every single day—when I looked over at the bottom right corner of Emma Kate's bulletin board, those words ran right up against my pride and bucked my strong sense of entitlement that I should get to follow Jesus on my own terms.

And I have no idea why I thought following my own spiritual counsel was a good idea. After all, I was the same person who'd decided that starving myself for the better part of ten weeks was a winning weight-loss strategy, and clearly that was some prime-time stupid.

But try though I did, I couldn't get away from the fact that the Lord was reminding me over and over again—through my sweet roommate, through her perfectly organized bulletin board, through the ways the Holy Spirit would prick my heart late at night when I wondered what real peace felt like—that somehow I was missing out on the joy of my salvation. And whether I liked those nudges or agreed with them or gave them my personal stamp of approval, the bottom line was that if I really and truly belonged to Jesus, He wasn't going to let me settle for a comfortable, convenient call of my own making.

Granted, a call that's comfortable and convenient would be, like, eleventy million times easier.

But thanks to Emma Kate's ever-present index cards, there was no escaping Paul's words and the near-constant reminder that I was going to have to make a choice—a real, grown-up choice—to fully embrace life in Christ by fully embracing the death of everything I thought I held so dear.

Because no matter how hard I insisted that I knew best, I couldn't seem to convince God to get on board with my plan to straddle the fence and content myself with lukewarm faith.

Apparently I'd severely underestimated the power of Emma Kate's whisper prayers.

CHAPTER 10

FRIENDS DON'T LET FRIENDS PLAN LATE-SUMMER WEDDINGS

So a funny thing happens in the South when people finish college.

Okay. Maybe it's not funny.

And maybe it's not just the South.

So let me start over.

Occasionally a particular thing happens in the South and also in other parts of the world when people finish college.

They get married.

You're welcome for the fact that I just took fifty words to say what I probably could have said in five.

And by the time I finished my undergraduate work at State, I felt like *everybody* was getting married. Now, I personally wasn't one of the people who was planning a wedding because, well, I'd never dated anyone seriously, and that's generally a pretty solid requirement for getting to the part where the guy of your dreams puts a ring on it, as my dear friend Beyoncé would say.

(I should clarify that Beyoncé and I aren't really friends.)

(Well, we were, but then she saw me do the "Single Ladies" dance and was basically consumed by white-hot jealousy. In my defense, however, it is hardly my fault that a French-cut leotard and I go together like rice and gravy.)

(Oh, I am a kidder who very much enjoys the kidding.)

Anyway. Yes. Weddings. Many of my friends were planning them. And back when I was young and fresh faced and well versed in the musical stylings of Wilson Phillips, the part that caught me off guard was that in addition to the general state of giddiness that goes hand in hand with celebrating a college friend's engagement and marriage, there was also a flip side: the inescapable realization that Real Life—it was nigh. It was impossible to ignore that there were all sorts of responsibilities and pressures just around the proverbial corner.

That sounds like Debbie Downer, doesn't it? I don't really mean it that way. Because listen—I love a good wedding. And I loved seeing my friends fall in love. And I loved getting to be a bridesmaid and participating in the wedding-related fun.

But inevitably, when the last of the rice or the birdseed or the rose petals had been thrown and I'd changed from my bridesmaid's dress and heels into sweats and Birkenstocks, I'd spend most of my drive back to wherever home happened to be at the time feeling like I didn't know what to make of my early twenties since they didn't look anything like what the Brat Pack movies of my high school days had trained me to expect.

I thought I could trust you, Rob Lowe and Demi Moore.

HOWEVER COMMA YOU LIED TO ME.

Because here's what I'd expected: a very grown-up life. I thought I'd drink fancy wine and maybe live in a historical townhome with an interior brick wall and a claw-foot tub in the bath. I pictured glowing success at a job that totally energized me and provided me with a deep reservoir of disposable income. I figured that surely—SURELY—I would have ironed out all the wrinkles in my faith. And most of all, I imagined that no matter where I lived, my closest friends from college would be right there with me, more than likely sporting some long, equestrian-print skirts and Adrienne

Vittadini sweaters as we wrapped up our days at a really nice restaurant like Olive Garden or TGI Fridays.

But, well, no.

So go ahead and make some wavy *Wayne's World* fingers. Sit back and relax. We're about to have ourselves a flashback.

• • •

The summer before my senior year at State, Elise and Paul got married. They did this because (1) they wanted to commit their lives to each other in a Christ-centered union, and (2) their hormones would not permit them to stay single any longer. They'd dated for three years, and since Paul had graduated at the end of our sophomore year, Elise took every summer school course in the free world (slight exaggeration) and finished her degree two semesters early. I have no idea how she managed to do this considering that she had a very lively social life, a job in the College of Engineering, and a time-consuming hobby as our personal etiquette consultant.

Okay. She wasn't really an etiquette consultant. But sister-friend knew her Emily Post backward and forward, and woe be unto anyone who decided to wear a hat after sundown ("You're protecting your face from what, exactly? The rays of the moon?") or don some white shoes after Labor Day ("WHITE BELOW THE BELT! We've got some WHITE BELOW THE BELT!"). I think all my friends would agree that it made sense for Elise to be the first one to get married; she had mama-ed all of us within an inch of our lives since our freshman year, and you only had to look at her and Paul when they were together to know that they were meant to be.

So August of my senior year, Elise and Paul had themselves a wedding. I think there were fourteen or fifteen bridesmaids, and we wore dresses that honest-to-goodness defy my fortysomething brain in terms of offering a description. I can only tell you to picture the busiest floral print you've ever seen in your life, place said floral print against a navy-blue background, and then wrap eighteen yards of that fabric around your body.

Then find yourself four more yards of fabric and wrap that around your shoulders.

The end.

We didn't so much wear those dresses as we were *enveloped* within them.

At the time, though, we thought those dresses were gorgeous. In fact, we thought everything about Elise's wedding was gorgeous.

(Hold on.)

(I cannot say that with a clear conscience.)

(Because I most definitely did not think that Elise's bachelorette party was gorgeous. It was fun, but it wasn't gorgeous.)

(Go ahead and make those *Wayne's World* fingers again.)

(It's time for a flashback within the flashback.)

(*Fancy.*)

• • •

Honestly, I don't know who in the world decided that we should go to New Orleans for Elise's bachelorette party. It was in New Orleans in July—and as far as I'm concerned, those two things should have nothing to do with each other. Certainly I understand that New Orleans has a reputation for great food and great music and a certain degree of, um, *mirth*, but none of that negates the fact that July and August are miserable down there. The humidity hangs from the sky like damp, musty sheets on an endless clothesline, and you can almost see the steam that hovers all along the riverbank reach out and attach itself to people as they weave their way through the French Quarter.

This sort of environment does not necessarily make me feel very festive.

But for Elise, I tried to be a good sport. I *wanted* to be a good sport. I plastered a smile on my face when we were getting ready to leave her parents' house for the drive to New Orleans, and I strategically picked a seat in the car that would provide me with optimal AC access.

I may have been young, but I was no fool when it came to proper summertime cooling techniques in the Deep South.

We reached the outskirts of New Orleans in a little over an hour, and I only had to look at the way the sun was hitting Lake Pontchartrain to know that it wasn't just hot—it was HOT. The water looked thick and still—like you'd need a scoop to put it in a bucket—and I started to dread all the walking we'd be doing that afternoon and night. Yes, I loved Elise like a sister, but New Orleans in July was going to call for a level of selfless sacrifice and surrender that I simply could not achieve in my own strength.

This was when I began to silently petition the Lord with a zeal I had not known since my high school days.

Dear Heavenly Father,

I realize I have been a little distant lately, what with all my questioning and stubbornness and insistence that You should really consider doing things my way. Forgive me for all that, Lord, and help me to trust You more.

Now. With all that out of the way, I really need to talk to You about this New Orleans in July business.

Lord, I love my sweet friend Elise. I'd do anything for her. I'd wash her clothes, I'd clean out her car, I'd write a seventeen-page term paper for her on the topic of her choosing. But, sweet Jesus, I do believe that this particular travel assignment is beyond me. Because, Lord, it is hot. It is humid. I am sweating through my clothes even as I offer up this humble prayer of desperation right here on the Twin Span Bridge. This level of perspiration DOES NOT BODE WELL, Lord, as I am currently completely inactive inside an air-conditioned vehicle.

Ohhhhh, heavenly Father, would you bind this heat? Would you consider providing a thunderstorm that might usher in a hint of a cool breeze? It doesn't even have to qualify as "wind." Just some movement in the trees, Lord. Yes, Lord. MOVE, Holy Spirit. Breathe on us. But not hot air, Lord. Breathe some cool air. Please. Sir. Lord. Jesus. Some cool, refreshing air. Just like, you know, you do in the mountains. We'd be oh so grateful.

In Jesus' name.

Now I know full well that the Lord *heard* my prayer, but in His sovereignty (I am using churchy language to hopefully conceal my lingering bitterness about the state of the weather that weekend), He opted to answer it differently from what I'd requested (continuing with the churchy language option). In fact, when we pulled up to our hotel, the air was so thick with humidity that the car windows fogged, and I braced myself for the wall-o-steam as I savored the car's last bit of air-conditioning and cracked open the door.

OH, MY SWEET FANCY MOSES.

All I could think of was a song I used to hear on *Hee Haw* when I was a little girl:

Gloom, despair, and agony on me
Deep, dark depression, excessive misery . . .

Not that I was being melodramatic or anything.

Our hotel rested under the shadow of the I-10 overpass on Canal Street, and I couldn't shake the thought that our parents would be horrified to know that we were spending the night at the intersection of Murder and Danger. After I grabbed my overnight bag from Elise's trunk, I side-eyed my way to the front door of the hotel, my mama's voice echoing in my head every step of the way: "Sophie, I just don't think I feel very good about this." In retrospect, I know we were probably at a solid seven on a safety scale of one to ten, but I think the heat was multiplying my paranoia and interfering with my ability to reason.

Clearly I was a real ray of sunshine that afternoon—you have probably picked up on that. But since I wanted to seize the day and savor the moment, I tried to think of ways to make it better. I remembered that when I was a little girl and would get ill as a hornet about the heat, Mama always used to tell me to go in the bathroom and run cold water over my wrists. I thought about trying that trick once we settled in our rooms, but I figured it would be like trying to put out a fire with a water gun.

After Elise passed out room keys, we rode the elevator up to the tenth floor. Since there were eight of us on our NOLA excursion, we'd hatched a plan to split the cost of two hotel rooms in order to keep the cost affordable. To our surprise, however, we unlocked our rooms and found that they came complete with two twin beds—not the two double beds we were expecting.

That meant we were going to have to either pay for two more rooms or sleep two to a twin bed.

We decided to go with the second option because, well, FLAT BROKE.

Marion and I shrugged our shoulders and threw our stuff on the same twin bed before I checked the mirror to see if I looked even remotely presentable for our night on the town. The short answer to that question was no. No, I did not, but since my hair and makeup didn't stand a chance against the humidity, I decided that I was as good as I was gonna get. My hair had frizzed into a modified version of Roseanne Rosannadanna's bob, but thanks to our efficient window unit, my shirt was no longer sticking to my back.

Progress!

Bring on the night on the town!

The insincere enthusiasm was in full force!

However, despite the heat, the humidity, and the uniquely noxious smell that is New Orleans in the summertime (I'm guessing I will not be asked to serve on a NOLA tourism committee at any point in the near or not-so-near future. I have made my peace with that; however, should they ever decide to do a campaign about traveling to New Orleans in the dead of winter, I can support that endeavor with my whole heart), we had the best time that night. We laughed our way down Canal Street, ate dinner at the Riverwalk, walked around in the French Quarter, sat and listened to some jazz music, and practically earned gold medals in the People-Watching Olympics of 1990.

When we finally started walking from the French Quarter to our hotel, it was technically early the next morning. Our late-night stroll through the Crescent City was at odds with the safety-first aspect of my personality, but I took comfort in the fact that I was sober as a judge and fully capable of screaming loudly for the authorities in the event of unforeseen danger.

And seriously, everybody else was just as clearheaded as I was. The point of our trip to New Orleans wasn't any sort of crazy debauchery; we just wanted to be together for a girls' night one last time before Elise became an old married woman. We recapped different stories from our night as we crossed streets with funny-sounding names—Toulouse, Conti, Bienville—and we broke into a light jog when we reached an abandoned parking lot that looked like the place where the word *sketchy* was coined. I hadn't necessarily counted on having to exercise, but I picked up the pace and took another opportunity to remind everybody that I'D NEVER EXPERIENCED HOTTER WEATHER IN MY LIFE.

I am nothing if not consistent in my feelings about the heat.

Once the hotel was in sight, we slowed down. One of Tracey's shoes had broken, so she hopped on Elise's back as we approached Canal, and I deliberately fell behind the pack and watched the other girls cross the street. Yes, I was hot (did I mention that?), but I was also awash in sentimentality (you can count on ole English major here to get all tenderhearted and reflective at the most inopportune times). I couldn't have pinpointed the moment when it happened, but during our time at State, the hearts of those girls had become so inextricably connected to mine that it was hard to know where one stopped and the next one began. We weren't unhealthy or codependent; heaven knows we tended to be straight shooters and quick to share our opinions. But we knew each other's hang-ups and struggles, and there was no enabling—oh, no ma'am. Even now I can hear Elise saying, "I get that you have some questions about the faith stuff, but at some point you've got to stop worrying about the parts you don't understand and just hop back on the dadgum train. ALL ABOARD, sister—the next stop is the CHURCH HOUSE, and it'll do you some good to pay a visit."

The Lord is mighty sweet to give us people who have no interest in attending our personal pity parties, you know?

It was equally as comforting that we knew the little stuff about each other too: who liked to twist her hair into loops when she was in deep thought, who had a pinky finger that didn't necessarily like to cooperate with all the other fingers, who put on her makeup like she was going to win a prize for finishing first, who memorized the previous year's Top 10 Miss Mississippi contestants' talents and could perform them on demand, who pointed the toes on her right foot when she was trying to decide what to wear in the mornings.

In so many ways, we were the first family we had ever gotten to choose. And now that Elise was getting married, it felt like the beginning of the end of an era.

In my humble opinion, that era was flying by way too fast.

I caught up with the other girls as they walked into the hotel lobby, and together—a bride and her tired, merry band of bridesmaids—we made our way to the elevator. We yawned and stretched and rested our heads on one another's shoulders, and I don't think any of us could shake the awareness that all we had waiting for us upstairs was half a twin bed. The elevator was obviously in no hurry to transport us to our cramped sleeping arrangements; we must have waited ten minutes for those doors to open.

When the elevator finally arrived, we—along with a few folks who had been standing behind us—shuffled our way inside and crammed ourselves shoulder to shoulder so we could fit. Elise, who was standing by the elevator panel, diligently looked from person to person and asked for his or her floor number. She was about to question a man who was standing in the center of the elevator when she paused for a second—and then a huge grin spread across her face. I turned to see what had caught her attention.

The man looked vaguely familiar, but I couldn't place his face for anything. He was wearing a tracksuit and more gold jewelry than I'd ever seen in one place, and I was just starting to hone in on his most noticeable piece of jewelry when Elise spoke up. Her smile let me know that she knew exactly who he was.

"Hey!" she said. "Why do you wear that big ole clock on a chain around your neck?"

The man's shoulders started to shake from laughter, and before he could answer, Elise said, "What floor, baby? You and that clock probably need to get on home."

His smile seemed to spread from one side of the elevator to the other, and his gold teeth glistened under the lights.

That's when it dawned on me: Elise had just made friends with Flavor Flav. On an elevator. At two o'clock in the morning.

Ladies and gentlemen, that right there is New Orleans in a nutshell.

• • •

Since being part of a wedding celebration was somewhat new to our group of college friends, Elise and Paul's wedding weekend was extra special. It

103

seemed mighty grown-up to stay in a hotel, go to the country club for a rehearsal dinner, nibble on dainty chicken salad sandwiches at the bridesmaids' luncheon, and gather in the church foyer for prewedding pictures with Elise. We'd spent the better part of three years living next to each other, crying on each other's shoulders, getting to know each other's families, and cementing our friendships over concerts and football games and late nights and fried chicken.

But then we blinked—and there was an actual bride among us.

The wedding was in the sanctuary of First Baptist Church, and between Elise's south Mississippi folks and Paul's people from the Mississippi Delta, you couldn't have squeezed two pennies onto any of the pews. That place was packed.

I didn't expect to be nervous as I walked down the aisle holding my arm bouquet of alstroemeria lilies, but I was surprisingly shaky and quivery and just the tiniest bit weepy. One look at Paul's face let me know that he was going to be an emotional wreck by the time Elise's sister, Christy—the maid of honor—walked down the aisle, so I took my place on the far-right side of the sanctuary, made sure my flowers were at the precise angle the wedding director had specified the day before, and waited for Elise to make her entrance.

To be honest, it wasn't a quick process. Between the bridesmaids, the flower girls, the groomsmen, and the clergy, there were about forty of us at the front of the church. There have been Mardi Gras parades with smaller processionals.

Finally, though, the back doors of the sanctuary opened, and Elise, holding tightly to her daddy's arm, walked down the aisle. Paul's chin quivered so much that I wondered for a split second if he might break it, and thanks to that funny way the brain tends to work at random moments, I ran through a four-second list of hypothetical questions: *Can a chin actually break? Would that require a cast? What if it needed a sling? Would an injured chin hurt every time it was about to rain?*

You can always count on me to hone in on the most important details. Once Elise took her place in front of her groom and the pastor, however,

I was dialed in. And twenty minutes later, she and Paul were husband and wife. Pledged, promised, vowed, and sealed with a kiss.

Paul bawled his eyes out through every single bit of it.

Elise pretty much smiled nonstop as she wiped away his tears.

● ● ●

For the next three or four years, that scene repeated itself over and over again. Sure, the churches were different, the bachelorette parties were different, and the ceremonies were different (nobody ever topped Paul Watson in the crying department; we should have given him a commemorative plaque), but the idea was the same: Wendi married Dave, Marion married Spence, Daph married Jimmy, Emma Kate married Brad, Tracey married Kirk.

(I would be remiss if I didn't mention that the heat *totally* overachieved at Tracey and Kirk's outdoor reception—so much so that Marion and I took it upon ourselves to go inside the house on the property and find a bedroom where we proceeded to hike up the skirts of our bridesmaid's dresses and stand over the air-conditioning vents for the better part of a half hour.)

(You might say that's ridiculous. But I say that it's resourceful.)

We seemed to move as a pack from one wedding to another to another to another, and I was increasingly aware that whether I liked it or not, we were heading into a new phase of our lives. Every time I watched another friend hop into a car with "Just Married" written in white shoe polish on the rear window, I felt an unavoidable pang of bittersweetness. I knew that it was right and good and normal for everybody to move into the next season, and I reminded myself that I was beyond fortunate to have spent four years with dear friends who had honest to goodness made me a better person. At the risk of sounding like a Hallmark card or, heaven forbid, someone on *The Bachelor*, they really had influenced my life in amazing, positive ways, and while I may not have had all my theology ironed out, I could still recognize that those sweet girls were living, breathing examples of God's faithfulness. They loved me unconditionally, they made me laugh, and they were a surefire guarantee that anything would be fun as long as we were together.

I was so grateful for that.

I was so grateful for them.

And even though change wasn't my favorite, it thrilled me to see my friends fall in love, especially since I adored all their husbands (I still do, mind you). An added blessing was that I didn't feel like I was just sitting around and biding my time until I could get married. I very much liked the perks of living by myself, chief among them being able to hibernate in my apartment on a wide-open weekend with an assortment of crackers, a couple of two liters of Diet Coke, and an entire season of *The Real World* on a VHS tape.

I don't mean to imply that Wheat Thins compare to marriage, of course. I'm just pointing out that my needs were relatively simple.

But still, there was one part of the "moving on" equation that I just could not reconcile.

I missed my people like crazy.

The fact that the whole equestrian-print skirt/Adrienne Vittadini sweaters/Olive Garden scenario wasn't going to work out was insult to injury, really. Granted, I wanted more for my friends than for them to be like Billy in *St. Elmo's Fire* and get stuck in a college-life mentality that leads to getting thrown out of bars and then leaving a family to go to New York and pursue a career as a saxophonist.

I just wanted to figure out a way that we could stay together, dadgummit. Maybe that meant we needed to build ourselves a subdivision with the world's largest cul-de-sac. And maybe there could be a screened-in porch that connected my house to Emma Kate's house so we could meet there every morning and evening and sit in a big ole swing and catch up on the news of the day. Maybe Wendi and Marion could share a deck with a built-in sound system that would make karaoke nights and pageant re-enactments a breeze. Maybe Elise, queen of the perfect playlist, could serve as our resident DJ, and Tracey, queen of the cheerleaders, could be our choreographer (doesn't every neighborhood need one of each?). And maybe Daphne and Katy could cochair our homeowners' association, because heaven knows those two could march into Congress on any given day and STRAIGHTEN OUT SOME THINGS.

(I could even picture an HOA notice written by Katy. It would say something along the lines of "MOW YOUR GRASS, FOOL.")

(Shakespeare may not have known her, but he sure enough described her: "Though she be but little, she is fierce.")

But a cul-de-sac wasn't going to be in our immediate future. And fortunately, I wasn't completely lacking a healthy, realistic perspective. I could recognize that the years in front of us were chock-full-o-possibilities. That certainly didn't change how much I missed everybody, but Mama had always told me that sometimes God doesn't give us what we want because He'd much rather give us what we need.

I tried to brace myself for whatever that might be.

And I prayed that it wouldn't involve another trip to New Orleans in July, oh Lord help us all.

CHAPTER 11

WHEN THE BELLS AND WHISTLES
BLOW UP AND GO *BOOM*

For most of college I drove a 1984 Buick Regal. It was maroon with a white vinyl top (of course it was), and though it was as long as half a city block, it was a two-door, which meant that each door extended almost the full length of the vehicle and weighed roughly eight hundred pounds apiece. Oh, you might *want* to slam those doors in a fit of anger, but the laws of physics made it all but impossible. The interior was soft maroon velour, and with its power windows, power locks, cassette player, and cruise control, Ye Olde Regal was, at least to me, a mighty nice car for my college days.

What the Regal was not, however, was reliable. It tended to sputter at red lights or stop signs, and after a few months of the stop-and-start traffic in Starkville, I learned to keep one foot on the gas and one foot on the brake so the engine wouldn't quit. It was also fond of refusing to go in reverse, which meant there were several times when I parked my car at a friend's apartment or at my dorm, and when I got ready to leave, I'd have to put the car in neutral and ask someone to push me backward. Eventually I learned the blessing of a pull-through parking space, but that wasn't possible at, say, Sonic—unless I was prepared to jump a couple of curbs and run over the metal picnic tables.

By my junior year, the Regal was in the shop with annoying regularity; if it wasn't the transmission, it was the catalytic converter, and if it wasn't the catalytic converter, it was the alternator, and if it wasn't the alternator, it was the battery. When I'd go home on the weekends, I'd sometimes have to swap cars with Mama or Daddy so the Regal could stay in Myrtlewood for repairs, but by the end of my junior year, I think Daddy was as tired of fooling with it as I was.

One of the Regal's more endearing qualities was that if I didn't want the engine to spit and backfire and quit, I had to drive at a sustained speed of at least thirty miles an hour. This was all fine and good until I found myself in a parking lot, where driving over, say, ten miles per hour was generally a really bad idea. In fact, one time I was at the mall in Columbus, Mississippi, when the Regal decided to die in front of McRae's department store, and when I finally got the car cranked again, I was so determined to get out of that parking lot and back on the highway to Starkville that I caught a wheelie you could have heard in three counties.

So basically what I'm saying is that the Regal lent a certain element of class and sophistication to my college years.

You'll just have to trust me when I tell you that you haven't lived until your vehicle has backfired in a jam-packed Taco Bell drive-thru.

The nail in the Regal's coffin was when it stopped running one day on Highway 82 between Columbus and Starkville. It's one thing to be an ongoing source of comic relief, but it had crossed over into "unsafe" territory. Daddy started looking for new (used) cars back home in Myrtlewood, and once I got home for summer vacation, I started throwing my ideas and opinions into the search.

I'm sure Daddy really appreciated my input. Especially considering that I was contributing approximately zero dollars to the transaction.

Daddy eventually decided on a car that I absolutely loved. It was Jeep's first foray into the car market—an Eagle Premier—and it ticked all of our boxes. Daddy liked it because it was an American car—a reasonably priced, seemingly sturdy sedan—and I liked it because it had all sorts of bells and whistles. The seat belts automatically positioned themselves when you closed the door, the blinker made a pleasant chiming sound, and the dashboard had a digital display that showed fuel economy, miles traveled, miles remaining on a tank of gas, etc. I've always liked a boxy car, and this one was just that; I imagined that I'd drive it for years and years to come.

Well.

You can pretty much guess what happened next.

After two or three months, the left axle—THE LEFT AXLE—needed to be repaired. On top of that, the fuses that controlled all those bells and whistles blew out so frequently that I not only carried spares in my glove compartment, I also knew how to install them. In fact, I did just that often enough that I contemplated adding a pair of coveralls to my wardrobe—complete with "Soph" embroidered over the pocket. The air conditioner quit working three or four times, the power steering went out, and those fancy seat belts developed an annoying habit of moving halfway into place—and then stalling. About a year and a half after we got the car, Mississippi had an especially hard winter, and when I hopped in the driver's seat one morning after a hard freeze, the little digital console thing wouldn't light up or turn on. It remained completely inactive until the next spring, when it lit up and started to beep one night on a drive from Jackson to Starkville.

I guess it finally thawed.

By year two I couldn't identify a single part of the Screamin' Eagle, as I called it, that hadn't been repaired—with the exception of the seats and the trunk (thank goodness the car was still under warranty; otherwise I imagine Daddy would have just driven it to the pasture and SET IT ON FIRE). It overheated at the drop of a hat, creaked like it was 105 years old, and randomly emitted loud, unpleasant noises. When David and I were dating, there was even one time when we were driving through a subdivision in Myrtlewood, and I KID YOU NOT, the front bumper fell totally off the car for no discernible reason.

Seriously. That bumper dropped it like it was hot. Right in the middle of Mission Hill Estates.

It was so par for the course that I didn't even panic. I just put the car in park, opened my door, asked David to help me pick up the bumper, and in about six seconds we had it snapped back on.

It was almost like I drove a Mr. Potato Head.

But here's the strangest part of all: despite all the trouble I had with that car, I loved it beyond reason. I knew every quirk it had—the way I could pop the horn off the steering wheel and honk it while it rested in my lap, the way I had to put cassettes in the tape player so it wouldn't immediately spit them out, the way I needed to position a piece of Tupperware on the passenger floorboard in case the air conditioner leaked—and I wasn't deterred by a single bit of it. Even though that car looked shiny and fancy on the outside, it was stubborn, it was temperamental, and it was prone to breakdowns.

On some level, I think I related to it. That car and I had more than a few things in common.

• • •

One Friday afternoon I drove to Myrtlewood to put my car in the shop for the sixth or seventy-ninth time. Since it wasn't fixed by the time I went back to school on Sunday, my daddy let me borrow his car for the return trip. He drove a beige Crown Victoria, which is basically a land yacht—exactly what every college girl fancies as her dream car.

This particular trip happened to coincide with what the modern-day church would call "a season of rebellion" in my life. My husband always tells me that when I talk about my early twenties, I make it sound like I was running a drug-smuggling ring and then murdering people in my spare time, so I want to be sure I don't overdramatize what I was dealing with. The reality is that a big chunk of my rebellion was straight-up selfishness with a whole lot of lying and sneakiness to try to get exactly what I thought I wanted. I told myself that I was way better than "other people" because I wasn't sleeping around or messing with drugs, but make no mistake: I was the most manipulative Pollyanna wannabe that you ever did see. I wasn't terribly concerned with the well-being of anyone other than me, myself, and I, and in addition to that, I can look back on some of the stuff I was reading and watching back then, and it's all too evident that I was increasingly comfortable with indulging my own darkness.

Bottom line: I was one stiff-necked somebody. Nobody could tell me anything since I thought I already knew it all (just ask Emma Kate, who tried and tried to get to the root of what was going on with me), and for the first time in my life, I felt cynical and pessimistic. My words were careless and disrespectful (not to mention that I'd developed significant affection for words that would have gotten me suspended when I was in high school), and since Scripture tells us that out of the overflow of the heart the mouth speaks (see Luke 6:45), it was pretty evident that a good portion of my overflow was dark, stagnant, and foul.

Okay. I might be on the verge of overdramatic mode again.

But you get the idea. Yes, there was part of me that was still a bow-headed sorority girl with incredibly sweet, loving friends. Yes, I was a people pleaser who cared a whole lot about what other people thought. But my issues weren't just *Oh my gosh, y'all, I have not had a quiet time in four days and I'm, like, SO SAD because I just miss Jesus SO MUCH.*

I was willingly sitting in some very real sin. And I was consistently wrestling with some very real shame.

It was late in the afternoon when Daddy's Crown Victoria and I hit the road to Starkville, and I was about fifteen miles into the trip when I started thumbing through his collection of cassette tapes. Daddy went on a big praise-and-worship kick in the early nineties, so there was no point in looking for the latest cassette single by Paula Abdul. There was gospel and there was praise music and there were collections of instrumental hymns with nary a Fresh Prince or DJ Jazzy Jeff song in the bunch.

After some deliberation, I finally picked up a greatest-hits album by the Maranatha! Singers and stuck it in the cassette player. Praise-and-worship music wasn't as widely used in churches as it is now, but I'd learned many of the choruses at high school church camp—and from listening to the music that Mama played in the kitchen when I was home.

For the first few songs, I halfheartedly sang along with words that I knew in my head but hadn't felt in my heart for several years. Eventually a song called "I Love You, Lord" started to play, and for reasons I still don't really understand, I only got as far as "I love you, Lord, and I lift my voice" before the words caught in my throat and I started to cry. Actually, I started to bawl. A flood of tears washed over me so quickly that I almost wondered where they'd come from; I had grown so accustomed to feeling jaded and hard hearted that the tears totally surprised me.

It occurred to me that I missed the days when faith seemed simple.

And I wondered what I'd done to mess it up.

Theologically I was way off the mark, of course, but it was easy for me to look at the sin and the rebellion and the manipulation in my life and just shrug my shoulders and tell myself that God had given up on me, that we'd had a nice little run for four or five years before I started to disappoint Him in countless ways. Like so many of us tend to do, I'd fallen into the trap of thinking that I carried the weight of the gospel on my shoulders—and then, as I drifted further and further from the One who had actually ordained every single bit of my life, I felt utterly embarrassed that I couldn't bear a burden that had never been mine to begin with. That kind of thinking sparks a strange, destructive cycle of spiritual defeat, and like a tornado, it picks up everything in its path—guilt, shame, hopes, doubts, fears—before it rips those things to shreds, scatters them across the landscape of our hearts, and somehow convinces us that we're on our own to pick up the pieces.

After all, if God really loved us, would He have ever allowed the storm?

But that afternoon, somewhere between Kemper County and Oktibbeha County, the Lord reminded me that even though "my flesh and my heart may fail . . . God is the strength of my heart and my portion forever" (Psalm 73:26). In all my brokenness I had my own little worship service in Daddy's Crown Victoria, and it was the sweetest reminder that even though I'd numbed myself to the joys of life in Christ, the Holy Spirit hadn't left me.

It probably goes without saying, but I was mighty relieved.

It's always good to remember that you aren't nearly as alone as you fear.

• • •

I would love to tell you that life was one big praise-and-worship chorus after my road trip in the Crown Victoria, but it wasn't. I still didn't have real community or true accountability, and I can't even say I had a genuine desire to turn from "the sin that so easily entangles" (Hebrews 12:1, NIV). I continued to hold tightly to the parts of my life where I didn't want God to have any say—lest He ask more of me than I was willing to give.

The illusion of control is a powerful thing.

It was a couple of weeks before the Eagle was out of the shop, and when I drove back to Myrtlewood, I found that I was a little reluctant to return the Crown Victoria to Daddy. Granted, nobody would have looked at his car and commented on its beauty, but it was sturdy and it was solid, and I knew firsthand that it was a safe place to be if you happened to be caught in a storm.

As soon as I sat in my car, though, I felt like I was home. The seat belt thingy still didn't work just right, and I knew it was only a matter of time before the engine overheated. I pushed a few buttons and levers to make sure the air and lights were working, and when I accidentally flipped on the turn signal, I noticed that its delightful, rhythmic chime had taken on a frantic quality, almost like a panicked little bird.

It was just one more thing to add to the list—and it made me laugh. Every once in a while, I reckon, broken stuff starts to feel downright comfortable.

The Screamin' Eagle and I made it back to my apartment without incident. I was grateful for it, but I knew better than to think that all our issues were behind us. History is a mighty good teacher, and that car had proved that it was high maintenance and unreliable over and over again.

But then again, so had I.

It didn't really make any sense, but for whatever reason, I continued to love that car—as much as a person can love a big hunk of metal and plastic, at least.

And you know what else didn't make any sense? The fact that, for whatever reason, God continued to love me.

But I'm so thankful that I knew He did.

CHAPTER 12

THE BRAT PACK MOVIES DIDN'T REALLY COVER THIS PART

I AM WELL aware that some people come into this world with a driving ambition and a steely determination to pursue their God-given talents no matter the cost or sacrifice. *Ain't no mountain high enough, ain't no valley low enough, ain't, no river wide enough*, etc. and so on and so forth.

I, however, was not born with that particular disposition. Plus, I grew up in the House Full of Practical People, so any grand, dream-chasing pursuit has always struck me as sort of pie in the sky. There have been a few odd occasions when I've decided to be bold and speak a goal out loud—something like, "Hey, I think I would really like to complete X, Y, and Z over the course of the next year"—but I'm inevitably embarrassed by how sidetracked I can get on the way to finishing what I've started. What's sad is that I can't even say I get sidetracked because I become superpassionate about something else. I get sidetracked because Bravo has a new show about wealthy British women or the SEC baseball tournament is in town or OH WAIT! OUR STEIN MART HAS BEEN REMODELED! WE HAVE TO GO!

I should probably be ashamed to tell you that I didn't even have to make up those examples.

So, since I'm not what you would call, um, *driven*, my daddy had the good sense to talk with me before I went to college so he could make sure I'd really thought through the process of deciding on a major. To my credit, I *had* given the subject some thought; for most of my junior year in high school, I was dead set on being a psychology major, but then my aunt Chox told me a story about a friend's daughter who got a degree in psychology and couldn't find a job anywhere in the country OR EVEN THE WORLD.

It may not have been quite that dramatic. But the thought of not being able to find a job was a serious deterrent. Even for me.

Once I'd put my psychology dreams aside, I shifted gears at the beginning of my senior year of high school and made up my mind that what I really wanted to be was an English major—which was clearly far more sensible than that psychology hogwash. After all, I think most of us know that when it comes to choosing a career, there are few fields more lucrative than the liberal arts.

I will pause at this juncture so you have ample time to guffaw and also chortle.

. . .

. . .

Daddy, who is one of the most sensible people I have ever known, was iffy about the English major and really wanted me to think in terms of what major would provide me with the most opportunities *after* college as opposed to the most enjoyment *during* college. It was a solid strategy, and I absolutely understood why he had reservations about English. He was reluctant, to say the least, to invest in four years of my college education so that one day I'd be able to quote an impressive array of poetry to my manager at the local Blockbuster Video.

I'd say he had some valid concerns.

So one Saturday morning, when Daddy and I were on the way to State for a football game, he called our college planning session to order and offered some counsel. The first major he suggested was computer science; since technology was growing by leaps and bounds and computers were becoming more common in people's homes, Daddy felt like I'd have my pick of jobs once I finished my degree. I didn't say anything as he made his case; I just nodded my head and pictured endless rows of ones and zeros and wondered what good it would be to have a job where I made a bunch of money if said job made me feel dead inside.

His second suggestion was business. Unfortunately, I am unable to summarize what he said, because I quit listening the second I heard the word *business*.

The third career option that he proposed was engineering. Mississippi State has always had a phenomenal engineering department, and thanks to their co-op program, most of their students have jobs lined up by spring of their senior year. I don't know that they have 100 percent placement, but it's close, and Daddy thought I'd have some incredible career prospects if I channeled my academic energy in that direction.

We sat in silence for a few seconds after he finished talking, and then I said something profound.

"But, Daddy, engineering requires a LOT of math."

"Well, that's okay," he replied. "You may just have to study a little harder."

I paused for a second before I responded.

"But, Daddy, I don't really *do* math."

"You can do anything you want if you put your mind to it," he said. He was trying so hard to stay positive, but I could see a hint of frustration along his jawline.

And I understood why. He wanted me to dream big and strive for excellence. It had to be challenging to try to motivate a child whose fallback strategy was to aim low. His intentions were great, but what Daddy didn't realize was that he was severely overestimating my academic ambition.

Plus, I'd loved to read and write my whole life. If the adage "The work you do while you procrastinate is probably the work you should do for the rest of your life" is true, then an English major was the only choice for me—limited employment prospects aside.

So that is what I did. I went to State and I majored in English and I never looked back. The only bump in the road was when I was a sophomore and decided I wanted to double major in English and broadcast journalism so I could work as a news producer like Jane Craig in *Broadcast News*. Certainly you could argue that it was somewhat foolish to add an extra eighteen months to my degree program just so I could imitate a fictional character in my real life, but I was blinded by the prospect of getting to work behind the scenes on a real-live news broadcast.

I clung to that dream for one whole semester.

Eventually I arrived at the conclusion that the idea of an extra year and a half of undergraduate work was deeply flawed—so flawed, in fact, that I skedaddled over to my adviser's office and reworked my schedule for fall. The double major was a lovely but shortsighted experiment. Daddy agreed—and asked one more time if I'd considered majoring in computer science.

Bless his heart. I couldn't help but admire his persistence.

● ● ●

Lee Hall houses the English department at Mississippi State, and when I was a student, room 312-B belonged to Dr. Mary Ann Dearing, who just so happened to be the director of teaching assistants, a certified Southern character, and my all-time favorite professor. Dr. Dearing's office was special because it had not one but two windows that looked out over Drill Field, and truth be told, it was critical to keep those windows cracked open at all times since Dr. Dearing smoked Parliament Lights like a stack. Her deep, raspy voice suggested that she and her Parliament Lights had been close friends for many years, and you'd better believe the friendship was still going strong. In fact, I never walked into Dr. Dearing's office when she didn't have a cigarette dangling out of the corner of her mouth or smoldering on the edge of an ashtray, and as soon as she'd see me standing in the doorway, she'd say, "Sit down, sugar!" while she slowly and noisily pecked away on her nicotine-stained keyboard.

I absolutely adored her.

Dr. Dearing fascinated me because she was such a twist on her generation's stereotypical Southern woman. She could certainly speak the language of the Junior League and the Daughters of the American Revolution, but she was also passionate about her career, outspoken in her opinions, and more than a little bawdy with her language. A creature of habit and discipline, Dr. Dearing pulled into her Lee Hall parking space at seven o'clock every morning, at which point she would step out of her car with a khaki-colored raincoat draped around her shoulders and a white thermal coffee carafe in her hands. She'd drink coffee in any form she could find it, but she was partial to Maxwell House French Roast with so much Cremora that the liquid in her Bear Bryant coffee mug resembled melted vanilla ice cream more than anything else. Throughout the day she'd pour cup after cup into that beloved mug, and between the coffee and the aforementioned cigarettes, she pretty much buzzed her way through whatever she needed to accomplish on a given day.

My pre- and post-class visits with Dr. Dearing, which started when I was a junior in her Advanced Composition class and continued through grad school, were often the highlight of my day, and I always walked away from her office with a little more knowledge than when I'd arrived. Dr. Dearing was full of anecdotes and theories and advice, and even though it has been almost twenty years since I last visited her office, I still remember the oddest assortment of her nuggets-o-wisdom:

- Girls either love horses or they don't. There's no in-between.
- Only children should wear red shoes.
- A beef bouillon cube is the key to a really good Bloody Mary.
- Rook is a delightful game.
- *Non sequitur* literally means "does not follow."
- Punctuation always goes inside quotation marks. ALWAYS, ALWAYS, ALWAYS.
- Respond to your students' papers as a reader. If a student writes an ill-constructed sentence about when her dog died, don't just mark "COMMA SPLICE" in red ink in the margin. Tell her that you're so sorry about the dog. The comma splice can wait.
- If someone repeatedly travels to Amsterdam on vacation, that person is probably not going to visit the landmarks and cruise the Rhine.

- There is no finer dessert than the black-bottom pie at Weidmann's in Meridian, Mississippi.
- If you want to keep your mind sharp, work crossword puzzles and play bridge.

Dr. Dearing consistently cracked me up; I'd never known anyone quite like her. But she also challenged me as a writer, and when she supervised my teaching assistantship in the English department while I was in grad school, she never hesitated to call me out and provide a much-needed come-to-Jesus moment when it was necessary.

It was necessary more often than I might care to admit.

Dr. Dearing did something else, too, though I don't know if she even realized it or gave it a second thought. She jumped all-in with her students, and even when she was so frustrated with them (or me) that she could have run screaming down the center of Drill Field with a cowbell in each hand, she never stopped cheering us on. She fought for us, she inspired us, and she really did love us to pieces.

• • •

One fall morning of my first year of grad school, I stopped by Dr. Dearing's office after I finished class. When I didn't immediately see her sitting behind her desk in her ancient roller chair (with tweed upholstery, no less), my first impulse was to leave. But since the door was open, the computer was on, and her beloved raincoat was hanging on the coat tree in the corner, I decided she must have walked down the hall for a few minutes. No harm in waiting, I figured.

I took a seat in one of the green vinyl chairs that always seemed to be occupied by one of Dr. Dearing's colleagues or a former student or a neighbor who was on campus and dropped by with a sack of fresh tomatoes (in Dr. Dearing's estimation, tomato sandwiches were a Southern art form, and she liked hers on white bread with mayonnaise, a touch of Durkee's, a smidge of salt, plus enough black pepper to season a porterhouse steak), and after I looked out of one of her windows to see if anyone I knew was walking across Drill Field, I turned my attention to the wall next to her desk.

At first glance, everything appeared to be standard professorial fare: a few plaques scattered here and there, some yellowed news clippings tacked to a bulletin board, a listing of English department phone numbers taped above her phone. But there were also mementos that spoke to who she was away from work: a snapshot of her beloved granddaughter on horseback, a group picture with dear friends, a comic strip that made her laugh every time she referenced it. I'm not really sure how to explain it, but there was an air of quiet achievement in that office. Dr. Dearing loved her family well, and she'd blazed a few trails in her career, but she hadn't sacrificed one on the altar of the other.

After several minutes I decided I'd just swing by again the next day, and I was about to grab my purse when a large white box caught my eye. It was about ten inches wide and twelve inches long, but please don't quote me on that because I believe I've already established myself as an unreliable source when it comes to numbers. I wondered what might be inside, and I quickly made a mental list of guesses.

Cookies?

A sweater?

Paperbacks?

Several cartons of Parliament Lights?

My money was on that last guess.

I knew full well that the contents of the box were none of my business. But I was twenty-two and stinkin' curious and also stupid. So I looked around to make sure no one was watching, and oh, Lord, forgive me, I opened that box.

I couldn't believe what I saw.

Because I instantly knew that it was a manuscript for a book.

There was a title page with an illustration and a byline on top of hundreds of sheets of white paper. I quickly thumbed through the stack of paper and saw double-spaced line after double-spaced line. Every sheet was full of her words, and while conscience stopped me short of skimming the content, that title page told me everything I needed to know: *Dr. Dearing had written a memoir.*

It didn't matter one iota to me whether the book had been published.

She'd written it. She'd finished a manuscript. And I thought that was extraordinary.

I'd never wanted to read something so badly in my life, but as fresh conviction washed over me, I gently put the top back on the box that was never mine to open in the first place. I picked up my purse and my backpack, took one last look at that white box, and left Dr. Dearing's office.

Chalk it up to guilt, cowardice, or a combination of the two, but I never told her what I'd done or what I'd seen. Granted, she probably would have gotten a huge charge out of the whole thing and teased me mercilessly for the better part of a year, but I felt like I'd trespassed over a boundary that should have protected a sacred part of her life and her heart. If she'd wanted me to know, she would have told me.

In my eyes, that manuscript catapulted Dr. Dearing to an even higher level of respect. The fact that she'd never mentioned it almost made me love her more.

So from that moment on, one aspect of my career path was settled: when it came to teaching and writing, I wanted to be just like Dr. Dearing.

Well, except that as a lifelong Mississippi State fan, I wanted nothing to do with a Bear Bryant coffee mug.

That probably goes without saying.

• • •

By the winter of the next year, most of my close friends were married and doing very grown-up things like buying houses or taking trips to the beach *without their parents*. I, however, was as single as ever, and I was hyper-aware that my days as a student were coming to a close. As a result, I knew I needed to find a job that paid real-live money—preferably something where I could earn more than the whopping $625 a month that I was raking in as a teaching assistant. To make matters worse, I was so burned out with school that I was behind in all of my classes and more committed to repeated viewings of *Melrose Place* than ever. Plus, that core group of friends that had surrounded and sustained me during college was scattered all over the state, and I missed the built-in accountability of their day-to-day presence like crazy.

There were people around me, of course. My childhood friend Kimberly lived across the hall from me, and our friend Gena lived in the building right next to us, but since they were both really dedicated students with serious boyfriends, they didn't have a whole lot of free time to hang out in my apartment and talk about the latest episode of *Seinfeld*. I very much enjoyed doing stuff with my friends Tracie and Rob, who were also grad students in the English department, but since they were, you know, *married to each other*, we'd mostly just go to lunch or supper and then hang out while we graded freshman composition essays that seemed to multiply in our backpacks.

So given all of that, I was alone a lot. A LOT. There was no roommate, no college friends nearby, no boyfriend. And while I have always been independent and enjoyed being by myself to some degree, I kind of took things to another level in grad school in terms of teetering on the edge of isolation.

Which reminds me.

One of the tricky parts of flirting with full-blown isolation is that it can be oddly enjoyable. Sure, it's sort of depressing, but it's also a great big Festival-o-Self. Like anything else, that festival gets old after a while, but you don't worry about that part so much when you're deeply involved in a two-day *Cheers* marathon with well-stocked supplies of chips, chocolate, Diet Coke, and Marlboro Lights.

Yes. You read that correctly. Because I think any professional counselor would tell you that if you're feeling sort of alone in the world, a surefire remedy is to FIRE UP SOME CIGARETTES. And here's the irony: I was terrible at smoking, yet I persisted with it for several months—almost as if I wanted to get to the point where someone rewarded me with a certificate of smoker achievement or something. I was such a smoker poser, though; I never really understood what was supposed to be enjoyable about it, and while I fancied myself a brooding loner, the fact of the matter was that I continued to wear oversize bows in my hair along with matching polka-dot sweater sets.

I'm not trying to perpetuate stereotypes, by the way. I'm just pointing out that my ongoing identity crisis manifested itself in some interesting ways.

And if my wannabe smoker status wasn't enough, I also made the rash (and some might say questionable) decision to get a cat. I KNOW. But a friend of Dr. Dearing's was moving to a place that wouldn't allow pets, and after she talked me into coming by and just "meeting" the cat, I agreed to take the cat home with me. It all happened over the course of about ten very impulsive minutes, and as I fought to hold on to my steering wheel while I drove down University Drive accompanied by an animal who, judging by her incessant hissing, couldn't have been less delighted about riding in a car, I knew that I'd made a terrible mistake.

So I did what most twenty-three-year-olds would do under similar circumstances.

I took the cat home and named her Prissy.

I don't even know what else to add to this story.

• • •

I'm only speaking from personal experience, of course, but when you're twenty-three and you have very few friends living in your town and you pretend to be a smoker and you own a cat, you might be tempted to wonder when the fun, grown-up part of your life is going to get cranked up and start moving forward. In my case, I alternated between telling myself I was perfectly content and then putting my hope in all sorts of ridiculously un-realistic scenarios, like how maybe that boy I had a crush on in high school would show up on my doorstep and declare his undying love, or maybe I'd be walking to class, lock eyes with someone who looked like Jake in *Sixteen Candles* (Jake is the pretend-boyfriend gold standard for Generation X girls), and get totally swept up in a whirlwind courtship, or maybe I'd tour the *Southern Living* offices in Birmingham, strike up a conversation with an editor, win her over with witty pop-culture references, and land myself a full-time internship where I'd get to type all manner of documents and sample food from the test kitchens ALL DAY LONG.

The occasional bout of desperation doesn't really breed realism, now does it?

My parents never confronted me about my general state of restlessness, and even now I'm curious if they knew what was going on with me during my early twenties—if they could see how I was struggling to figure out who I was and what I believed. But I do know this: smack-dab in the middle of the literal winter of my discontentedishness (totally a word)—and probably in the middle of watching *Real World: New York* when I should have been grading essays—Daddy called and said that he and Mama wanted to send me to a weekend retreat that had meant a great deal to them when they'd attended several years earlier. I agreed to go because I didn't want to disappoint them, but in the back of my mind I wondered what in the world I was going to do for a whole weekend at a campground outside of Jackson, Mississippi, where I would probably be the youngest person by a mile, people would talk about Jesus nonstop, and I wouldn't be able to smoke like a sorority girl (quick inhale, exasperated exhale, then repeat).

I mean, give me a little credit. Because despite all of my issues, I still had the good sense to know that it was tacky to smoke at a church camp.

And for the record, I'm certain that there have been some lovely, God-fearing smokers at church camps throughout the years. I am just trying to communicate my twenty-three-year-old thought processes, flawed though they may have been.

I don't remember many specifics from that weekend at Camp Garaywa, but I do remember my Big Takeaways:

- I had a lot to learn about living a life of faith.
- I had a lot to learn about the Bible.
- I had a lot to learn about God's character.

BUT.

- I knew that I *wanted* to learn.
- And I knew that I loved Him. Still.

This felt like significant progress.

It's interesting in retrospect because it was so unexpected, but Camp Garaywa was the first thing that had ever made me ready to leave Starkville. In fact, I was so camped out on the mountaintop experience of Jesus! and love! and joy! that I actually had a hard time going back to Starkville when the retreat was over. Instead I drove to Mama and Daddy's house, called Dr. Dearing, and told her I wasn't going to be able to make it to

Tuesday's classes. I finally drove back to Starkville that Wednesday, kicking and screaming my way down a significant stretch of Highway 45.

I'm pretty sure I must have missed the memo about doing my work as unto the Lord.

And clearly, Jesus and I had a few more kinks to work out in terms of my views on personal responsibility.

Considering how I had struggled with feeling like I was stuck in the in-between while everyone was moving on with their lives, I was almost relieved when I left Camp Garaywa knowing that it was time for *me* to move on too. I still needed a couple of classes to complete my master's, and there was an unfinished paper hanging over my head, but I wanted to find a job and move into the next phase of my life. On one hand, I knew that grad school had been worth it because it had made me a better writer, but on the other hand, grad school had been so challenging emotionally and spiritually that I couldn't wait to get the heck out of Dodge.

Or Starkville, as it were.

Unfortunately, I didn't have the foggiest idea where to go.

• • •

The following spring was a disaster.

Just trust me on that.

Okay. Fine. I'll provide an embarrassing detail.

Early in the semester I'd developed a very large crush on the man who is now my husband. It hit me out of nowhere considering we'd been friends practically all our lives. I even remember one specific time when he stopped by my apartment, and as soon as he walked through the door, I thought, *Oh. He is VERY cute. What is different about him? Why do I have a sudden urge to giggle? Who am I, and what is happening?* However, since David and I were just really good friends, there were a thousand potentially awkward moments standing between us and a dating relationship.

But I could not stop thinking about the possibility of a dating relationship.

And, well, thanks to the crush and a large dose of academic apathy, I basically lost all interest in school. Oh, I taught my classes, and I (mostly) went to my classes too. But I couldn't seem to muster the will to complete my assignments, especially for a class called Utopian Literature. Part of the reason I struggled in that particular class is because—and you heard it here first—Utopian Literature is a drag. Still, though, I should have made more of an effort. At the very least I could have tried to *appreciate* the genre even if I didn't enjoy it.

Anyway, there were three or four papers due throughout the semester, and I never wrote a single one. NOT A SINGLE ONE. I pretty much just sat in my apartment and wondered what china I would pick out if David and I ever decided to date because obviously if we started to date we would eventually get married and register for china and CLEARLY THIS WAS MY PRIORITY, PEOPLE. So at the end of the semester, when I had basically failed to participate in the class in any meaningful way, the professor put a beautifully handwritten note in my English department mailbox. Here's what it said:

I'm sorry that you were unable to submit any papers for grading.
Course grade: F.

Isn't that just about the nicest F you've ever heard of in your life?

I mean, seriously. That professor could have said so many mean things to me, like *Way to go, Super Slacker!* or *I didn't realize you needed directions to the computer lab!* or *Good luck with your pretend boyfriend!*—but for whatever reason, he was mercifully kind. Lord knows that I've carried that F around in my heart for a lot of years, but whenever I think about it, I'm inevitably charmed by the way my professor delivered the news.

So I guess maybe that's the bright spot?

And anyway.

Spring = disaster.

Moving on.

• • •

By the time summer rolled around, my employment prospects were drier than a bone. I wouldn't necessarily say that I was panicked about my lack of potential income for the fall, but I was beginning to feel anxious. I wasn't making a lick of progress with finding a job, and I'd started to think of countless unrealistic scenarios in terms of what I might be able to do to earn a full-time salary:

- I could be a full-time proofreader at my aunt and uncle's printing company even though they had no need for a full-time proofreader.
- I could move to Nashville and work as my sister's personal assistant even though she had no need for a personal assistant.
- I could buy foreclosed houses for pennies on the dollar, refurbish them, and then sell them at a significant profit even though I had no real estate experience (I'm pretty sure this idea came from a late-night infomercial, and I'm also pretty sure that a Tony Robbins infomercial that followed the foreclosure infomercial is what convinced me that I'd be fantastic at the real estate stuff because I just needed to BELIEVE IN MYSELF).
- I could babysit full time even though the kids I'd babysat during the summers were now in elementary school.
- I could open up a bookstore/greeting card store in my hometown even though I had upwards of seven dollars in my checking account and had no idea how to run a business.

So the future—it looked very promising!

I had so many great ideas!

Please pardon me, and in the words of DJ Kool, "let me clear my throat."

Ahem.

But in the midst of all that, here's what I really did know way down deep in my soul, even when I tried to push it out of my mind: I wanted to be an English teacher. I kept thinking about Dr. Dearing's example—about the way she loved her students and shared stories from her life and told us the truth when she graded our papers. I thought about how, when I looked back on grad school one day, I'd probably remember the hard times more than the happy times, but I'd also remember the near-constant encouragement and humor from the five-foot-two-inch dynamo with a smoker's cough, an impressive array of shirtwaist dresses, and a deep, unshakable affection for place and for people.

The irony, of course, was that as far as I could tell, no one was actually *hiring* English teachers that summer. And despite Daddy's noble attempts to steer me into a field that might be more lucrative, neither of us could have anticipated the impact of spending three years with a professor as gifted and hilarious and wise as Dr. Mary Ann Dearing. Yes, I valued her feedback on my writing and my teaching—and I admired her dedication to her own writing—but more than anything else, I treasured her friendship. And I wanted an opportunity to pass along what she'd taught me.

Well, maybe not that little tidbit about Bloody Marys.

But everything else?

Golden.

CHAPTER 13

NO ME GUSTA, Y'ALL

As long as I live, I will never forget the morning I drove to a "real" job for the first time. Considering the drive only lasted about two minutes tops, there's not all that much for me to remember, but maybe that's precisely why it's still so fresh in my mind more than twenty years later.

For starters, I was scared beyond all reason. Like, *terrified*. I didn't have a really strong frame of reference in terms of what to expect, and the constant flip-flops in my stomach reminded me that I was headed into a day full of unknowns. I half wished my car would break down so I could delay the inevitable, but the Screamin' Eagle was in fine form. Or maybe I should say it was in normalish operational form. Because most people rightfully expect that their cars will travel eight-tenths of a mile without incident. Perhaps I was a smidge jaded in the area of transportation.

I was also somewhat traumatized by how early I had to wake up. I'd spent the last six years on a college student's schedule, so when I passed by a crew of workers from the power company who had obviously been hard at work for a couple of hours, I wanted to honk and salute and thank them for their selfless service. It only took one early morning to make me realize how SPOILED DANG ROTTEN I had been in terms of my sleeping habits, and I felt a sense of solidarity with all the faithful employees who had been heeding the call of their alarms for fifteen, twenty-five, or maybe even fifty years.

The morning I remember so well was going to be my first day teaching high school students, and I dreaded it with everything in me. Since I'd been an English major and not an English education major, I'd never taken any classes in classroom management or disciplinary methods or anything like that. I'd taught freshman composition for four semesters, so I wasn't unfamiliar with talking in front of people, but a college classroom and a high school classroom are two totally different animals.

And from my perspective, at least, the former was an older golden retriever, while the latter was more of a rabid honey badger.

Not that I was judging, of course.

So all that to say: my mind-set going to work that morning wasn't exactly positive. I was flop sweat–level nervous, I was way too emotionally invested in the dedication of the power company workers, I was frustrated that my car worked, and I was dreading the reality of spending the next nine months in a den full of honey badgers.

And, well, there was one other teeny tiny little thing.

I wasn't teaching English.

Yep. You heard me. But I'll say it one more time just in case it's helpful for that tidbit of info to sink in for a few seconds.

I wasn't teaching English.

Oh, people. There's something so tricky about the best-laid plans.

● ● ●

I don't think there was anything particularly irrational about assuming that if I ever got a teaching job, it would be in English. I certainly hadn't applied to teach in other disciplines, and while I knew I wasn't the strongest student in the English department at State (say it with me now: "I'm sorry you were unable to submit any papers for grading"), I had hoped that my teaching evaluations from Dr. Dearing would open a door or two. Ultimately, though, I limited my options by deciding I had to be near my hometown. I didn't want to teach anywhere that was more than fifteen minutes away from Myrtlewood, and while I could tell you that was because the Lord was clearly leading me in that direction, the truth is that I wanted to live closer to David.

It's such a long story. Here is the shortish version:

- Boy and girl are friends their whole lives.
- Boy and girl are inseparable during college.
- Boy leaves Starkville after graduation and works in Myrtlewood.
- Girl stays in school in Starkville.
- Girl misses boy.
- Boy misses girl.
- Girl thinks she has a crush on boy.
- Boy thinks he has a crush on girl.
- Girl spends several months wondering, *WHAT DOES IT ALL MEAN?*
- Boy spends several months watching *Die Hard* on laser disc when he's not at work because why would he stress out over a crush?
- Boy and girl start to talk about the possibility of dating.
- Girl panics and decides it's now or never and she'd better move close by or they'll never date ever and what if he's supposed to be her husband and how could she miss that and she doesn't want to risk moving far away.
- Boy continues to watch *Die Hard*.
- Girl confines job search to a ten-mile radius of her childhood home; parents shake heads at her foolishness.
- Boy tells girl that she shouldn't move just for him; they have plenty of time, and she should go wherever she wants to go.
- Girl tells boy that she only wants to be in Myrtlewood; she'd never live anywhere else, and she can't think of any place that could be better for a twenty-three-year-old!

- Girl sits by the phone a lot and waits for someone to call her for an interview.

About six weeks before school was scheduled to start, I picked up the phone on a whim and called the principal of Myrtlewood High School. Mr. Pearson was one of the assistant principals when I was in high school, and our families have been friends for years. He's a kind, soft-spoken man who loves the Lord and always offers a timely word of encouragement, so calling him didn't feel nearly as awkward as it would have if I'd been calling a complete stranger. He answered his phone on the second or third ring, and after we exchanged a few pleasantries, I buried the lead.

"W-w-w-well," I stammered, "I know you didn't have any English positions back in the spring, but I'm still looking for something, and I was just wondering if anything has changed? Has anything opened up for fall?"

"I tell you what, Soph," Mr. Pearson answered. "I still don't have anything in English for fall."

My heart sank.

But then he continued. "However, I *did* have something open up in another department, and you're probably not interested, but—well—can you teach Spanish?"

"Spanish?" I asked.

"Yep. Spanish," he responded. "It would mainly be Spanish I—maybe a couple of classes of Spanish II—so if you're interested, we'll have to get you a temporary teaching certificate, but I'm happy to give you a shot."

My brain went into overdrive. I'd taken four semesters of Spanish as an undergrad, so I was a decent Spanish *reader*, but as far as speaking? It had never been my strong suit. Plus, I'd have to teach other people how to speak, and I just didn't know if I'd be able to do that.

Suddenly, though, I remembered my own Spanish I class in Myrtlewood, and I thought about the stuff we learned: numbers, alphabet, vocabulary, short dialogues, verb conjugations. I felt pretty solid in those areas. Plus, we had fiestas once a semester and listened to Mexican folk music while we ate chips and queso. Compared to analyzing literature, teaching Spanish might be a nice way to ease into working with high school kids. And before I had a chance to consider the cons of taking a job that was outside my subject area, I broke the silence.

"You know what? That sounds GREAT, Mr. Pearson!"

There was most likely, probably, quite possibly some insincere enthusiasm in my response.

"I'll get the folks in the personnel office to set up your contract," he replied. "Just give them a call the next time you're in town, and they'll go over what we need to do about certification."

"I'll definitely do that," I responded. And then I remembered my manners.

"Hey, Mr. Pearson, thank you so much. I can't even tell you how much I appreciate this."

"Well, I'm glad it's worked out. You are mighty welcome."

And that, my friends, is how I made the switch from prospective high school English teacher to la profesora de español.

It was as easy as *uno, dos, tres.*

• • •

I've never really been a fan of the whole "fake it till you make it" philosophy, but that mind-set was my lifeline for my first semester as a Spanish teacher. I got off to a rocky start because I'd underestimated how difficult it would be for me to establish authority as a twenty-three-year-old in a room of sixteen-, seventeen-, and eighteen-year-olds. Every single mistake I made with classroom management came back to bite me; I'd given the kids such a specific, exhausting list of classroom dos and don'ts that they immediately looked for loopholes to see what they could get away with. I'd been so adamant that *these are the rules that you absolutely have to follow* that I didn't allow myself any wiggle room for plain ole common sense.

This was never more evident to me than one morning when I was a few minutes late to my third-period class. I'd run down to the office after second period because, well, Mama called me. This was back before everybody had a cell phone, and sometimes, when Mama felt like she really needed to tell me something, she'd call the school secretary—whom she'd known for twenty years, probably—and ask the secretary to page me over the intercom. When Mrs. Griffin would remind Mama that I was in class, Mama would say, "Oh, that's okay! I'll just hold on. Thank you *so much!*"

So inevitably Mrs. Griffin would page me over the intercom and say, "Miss Sophie? Can you run down here and take a phone call from your mother on line two?"—and I'd immediately leap to the worst-case scenario in my head. I'd walk to the office wondering who had died or what terrible tragedy had befallen our family, and when I'd pick up the receiver and try to collect myself before I listened to what was sure to be life-altering news, Mama would start talking:

"Sophie? You having a good day? Now, I know you're probably not ready to start thinking about this just yet, but I was talking to Chox earlier this morning, and we decided that we want to have a cookout at Dalewood this Sunday after church. Just family—nobody else. Chox and Joe have been repainting the lake house, but it should all be finished by then, and we just thought it might be fun to cook hamburgers and visit. What do you think?"

"MAMA. I THOUGHT SOMEBODY WAS DEAD."

"Oh, heavens no. Sorry I scared you! I'm just making my grocery list and wondered if you could bring the potato salad."

"Yes, ma'am. I'll bring the potato salad. And please let me reiterate that I THOUGHT SOMEBODY WAS DEAD."

"Everything's fine! Your daddy's on the golf course, and I'm gonna run to Winn-Dixie in an hour or two. Have you talked to your sister or your brother?"

"Yes, ma'am. I talked to both of them last night."

"Oh, good. Glad y'all could catch up. Well, I know you need to go to class, so be sweet! Love you!"

It usually took a minute or two for my heart rate to return to normal.

On the morning when Mama's phone call made me late to third period, I was only halfway up the stairs when I realized there was a lot of commotion inside my room. When I finally walked in the door, the noise died down, and a precious, sassy girl named Shay was sitting on top of a desk, looking at me out of the corner of her eye and grinning like the Hamburglar.

Shay had a huge crush on a boy named Kito, and her preferred method of flirting was to antagonize him. She'd try to trip him when he walked by her desk, she'd pop him on the side of the head if she disagreed with him, or she'd contradict whatever he said just for the fun of it. I don't have any idea what they were "arguing" about while I was on the phone with Mama, but I do know that as I turned my head from Shay's impish grin to the chalkboard at the front of the room, this is what I saw written in all caps—in bright-pink chalk, no less:

KITO SMELL LIKE FART

I probably would have gotten a lot madder if Shay hadn't been so proud of herself.

Plus, I was deeply—DEEPLY—tickled, only I couldn't let it show. I made a big production of erasing the board to buy some time, and when I finally composed myself enough to reprimand Shay for her choice of words as well as writing on the chalkboard without permission, she grinned even wider. Her big hazel eyes were practically dancing with mischief, and when I was finished, she spoke up.

"Okay, Señorita," she said, invoking a fairly ridiculous way to address someone who often gave the word *casa* four syllables of distinctive Southern flair. "I won't do it again. But I didn't know I was doing anything wrong because . . ."

HERE IT COMES.

". . . you never said, 'Don't write on the chalkboard' on that list of classroom rules."

THERE IT IS.

And please, by all means, if you'd like to draw up a flowchart or something to illustrate how I was trying to make my students live under the letter of the law JUST LIKE I'D ALWAYS TRIED (and failed) TO DO, have at it. It would be a good while before I realized that you only need about four general guidelines to create and maintain an orderly, fun learning environment. But one of my biggest teaching flaws was that I tended to focus more on the kids' behavior than on their hearts, and for better or worse, that's where I found myself with Shay.

I took a deep breath before I responded to her.

"You're right, Shay. I have never specified that you couldn't write on the chalkboard. I'll give you a pass on that one. But I'm still gonna take issue with the use of the word at the end of your sentence. It's not a kind thing to say."

Shay folded her arms as the grin disappeared from her face. I could feel every set of eyes in that classroom watching us.

"And besides," I said, "the English major in me can't let go of the fact that you have a subject-verb error in your sentence. Because if I were your English teacher, I'd totally take off three points for that 'Kito smell' business."

See? I was a nit-picking, petty woman. I had let my guard down, and my real personality came out, and I could only imagine that I was about to have full-blown mutiny on my hands.

Shay continued staring at me for five or six endless seconds, and then, much to my surprise, she laughed. "I'm sorry, Señorita. I shouldn't have written that."

"Th—I mean, *gracias*," I replied. "Now apologize to Kito, please. Um, *por favor*."

"Sorry, Kito," Shay said.

He lifted his chin toward the ceiling in acknowledgment.

Then Shay spoke up again.

"Wa-aaait a minute! I forgot to say it this way: *Lo say-in-toe mucho*."

Then she winked and gave me a thumbs-up. I was rattled as all get-out, but there was no room for recovery time. I had to start the day's lesson.

At some point, I hoped, I'd get comfortable with the disciplinary stuff. But I couldn't imagine when it would be.

• • •

When I was in high school, I never, ever thought about how emotionally exhausting the days must have been for my teachers. I know it's typical for students to assume that their teachers have no life outside of school, and I well remember those awkward moments when I'd run into, say, my biology teacher at the grocery store. It always took a few seconds to process a sighting of a creature outside its natural habitat, and then the most mundane implications of seeing Mrs. Coleman in the produce aisle, for instance, would just blow my mind.

She shops.

She eats.

She prepares food for her family.

It was like watching an episode of *Wild Kingdom*.

I quickly learned, though, that being on the other side of the podium was no joke. In fact, there were lots of days when I'd step out in the hall-way between classes, walk down the stairs next to my room, then stand underneath those stairs and cry for thirty or forty-five seconds before I went back up to my room. The emotional ups and downs were significant; I was trying to find my way in terms of earning the respect of my students, and as far as that part of the job was concerned, it wouldn't have mattered if I'd been teaching Spanish or English or molecular biology (AS IF). We had a diverse student population, and while that meant my days were never, ever boring, it also created some challenges. The kids' resentments and judgments and jealousies often bubbled to the surface.

From that perspective, teaching Spanish was the easiest part of my job. Granted, my accent was terrible (this shouldn't be a surprise considering that on my best days I sound like a cross between Elly May Clampett and Minnie Pearl), but I'd forgotten that in Spanish there's an initial fascina-tion with the language—at least for most people—that lasts for two or three months. We recited the alphabet and practiced vocabulary words and worked our way through the textbook. Some days I was a hot mess and on the verge of a nervous breakdown by fifth period (my biggest lesson about teaching high school kids: yelling at them doesn't solve a thing; it just makes them defensive). Some days the kids tried to take advantage of me and push my patience to its limit. Some days I'd plan a lesson that turned out to be as boring as dirt, so I'd punt and let the kids watch *The Lion King* in Spanish. Again. Even though they didn't understand a word.

I told myself that's what subtitles were for.

Gradually, though, there were two or three good days for every five or six bad ones. The kids and I started to figure out each other's personali-ties. Most—though not all—of the troublemakers decided to at least try to trust me, and I tried to stop micromanaging them. I definitely wasn't anything special when it came to teaching Spanish. In fact, if I saw any of those students today, I would probably apologize for not being a better teacher (and in case you're wondering, I would apologize in English, not Spanish—because I probably wouldn't remember how to say that whole sentence in Spanish). Nonetheless, I was totally surprised by how deeply I cared for those kids. Their stories fascinated me and broke my heart and made me laugh until I cried.

By the time February rolled around and first-semester exams were behind me, I felt like I just might make it until May.

Muy bien, right?

• • •

One of the very best parts of being back in Myrtlewood was that I got to work with a lot of the people who had been my junior high and high school teachers when I was in school. Initially it was the strangest thing to sit in the teachers' lounge with, for example, the person who'd taught me trigonometry and calculus and try to will myself to call her by her first name ("Deborah," I'd silently practice. "Deb." "Deborah."), but after a few weeks, I started to adjust. I would forever see those women as my teachers, but to my surprise, I also started to see them as my friends.

And here's the part that sort of makes me want to claw my eyes out when it's late at night and I'm thinking about all my early twenties new-teacher bravado.

Looking back, I can absolutely see how immature I was when I would sit in that teachers' lounge and share all the thoughts and theories and grand realizations that had occurred to me in all of my SINGLE-DIGIT MONTHS of teaching high school. Most of the women (and the reason that I'm specifically mentioning the women is because I didn't really hang out with the men) I ate lunch with every day had been teaching for at least fifteen years—some for twenty, twenty-five, thirty—so clearly it would have served me way better to ZIP IT and sit back and listen.

But what has occurred to me—as recently as the last four or five years, even—is that while I didn't always listen, I watched those women like they were a Jason Bourne movie and I was afraid to turn away lest I miss a critical plot twist. I watched how they managed to stay laid back and low key no matter what was going on. I watched them use humor to win over the kids and diffuse just about any situation. All those ladies seemed to have a knack for mothering the young'uns who resisted authority, and when it came to sports and extracurriculars, they rallied behind those kids like nobody's business. Their thoroughness and consistency spoke volumes to me, and while they didn't talk about Jesus when they interacted with their students, their diligence and patience made it so evident that their work was their ministry.

I don't know. It's tough to make generalizations about what every young teacher needs—and I'm aware that many, unlike me, make a seamless transition from college to the classroom. But in my opinion, it would do most beginning teachers a world of good to spend a couple of years in the kind of company I had in that teachers' lounge. At different points as a new teacher, I flat-out blew it; I made a ton of mistakes and a slew of bad decisions, all thanks to my arrogance and my stubbornness and my insistence that I knew better.

But those women.

Those women.

Their examples taught me so much about the stuff I didn't think I needed to know.

And it's not lost on me that when I started working at Myrtlewood, I thought I was just taking a job.

But as it turned out, I was getting myself an education.

There are just some things that college can't teach you, I reckon.

• • •

The classroom wasn't the only place where I was in the dead center of a learning curve—because those were some strange and trippy days in my personal life. And they weren't "trippy" because I was embracing my inner flower child, mind you; I have been terrified of drugs ever since I was eleven or twelve and saw a made-for-TV movie where Helen Hunt tried PCP and then, in the middle of a hallucination, jumped out of a second-story window. That was pretty much all I needed to know to take a "NO THANK YOU, I DON'T BELIEVE I WILL" stance with illegal substances.

Every once in a while being a hybrid of a chicken and a scaredy-cat comes in handy.

But of all the stages of life I've experienced so far, those early working years were the weirdest. Technically I was doing things that adults do—paying rent, going to work, grading papers, even showing up at church occasionally—but I was constantly wondering what might be next. Some days I felt like I was back at the Clarks' house "playing teacher" with Kim, and I think a lot of that was because I was living in my hometown. Life there was familiar and easy, to a certain degree, but nothing felt long term, much less permanent. My college friends weren't there, and even though several of them had started their families, I wondered if I'd forever feel unsettled without them in my day-to-day. Plus, I was still very much known as Bobby and Ouida's daughter—which was fine and good and wonderful—but it was hard for me to figure out new boundaries with my parents. I vacillated between craving their approval and their pats on the back—and then trying to convince myself I shouldn't care so much about what they thought.

(Here's a hot tip to twenty-four-year-old me: just go ahead and accept that you will most likely *never* stop craving the approval of your parents, and as you get older, it doesn't matter if you dig a ditch, have a baby, write a book, win an award, WHATEVER—you still want to hear your parents say, "I'm proud of you. You did a really good job.")

(Whether or not you actually did a good job will be completely inconsequential. You will be totally content with lip service.)

(Good talk.)

I kept thinking that I should feel completely at home in Myrtlewood; after all, everything was familiar, from friendly faces at the grocery store to folks in their perma-pews at church to the rhythm of the red lights on Mission Hill Drive. Gradually, though, I started to realize that even though Myrtlewood hadn't changed that much in the seven years since I left for college, I had. I needed to figure out a way to be comfortable in my own space—which had a lot more to do with the interior of my heart than with my proximity to my old stomping grounds.

And then, in addition to all that, there was the David factor—which, come to think of it, sort of sounds like a TV show about people who learn to demonstrate extraordinary courage in seemingly impossible situations. Like, for instance, when fighting with a giant.

Please know that I'm just as sorry as I can be that my brain works like it does.

Anyway.

David and I did start dating after I moved back to Myrtlewood, but in the grand scheme of things, our relationship lasted about a minute. Well, maybe six minutes. I was very insecure—with a flair for the dramatic, no less—so we bickered way more than I think either of us had expected. Eventually we had a huge fight because I lied to him about something stupid, and that argument only reinforced the idea that the recurring theme for our dating relationship was WE ARE NOT READY FOR THIS. David was more accepting of that truth than I was, so after we broke up, he threw himself into his new job while I basically modeled my life after a heartbreak montage in an after-school special. I wrote lengthy journal entries by candlelight, I bundled up in oversize sweaters and stared into space, I listened to old Anita Baker albums, and I sang through my tears when I'd hear "Ghost" by the Indigo Girls.

Needless to say, I did not see our parting of the ways as an opportunity to deal with my propensity for high drama.

I couldn't even watch *Friends* without thinking, *I RELATE TO RACHEL'S FEELINGS FOR ROSS SO MUCH, Y'ALL.*

It was the winter of my second year at Myrtlewood High before I started to have some healthy perspective about the breakup (better late than never, I suppose). I could totally see that I'd expected my relationship with David to magically make me happy and somehow erase all the internal questioning and doubting and wrestling that had marked the previous five or six years.

But hindsight had helped me realize something I've never forgotten: it's no fair to hold a man responsible for fixing something he had no part in breaking.

And there just comes a point, I reckon—a crossroads—when it's time to get honest with the Lord and yourself and move forward in the process of becoming a real-live grown-up.

You can imagine my surprise when I realized that was exactly what I intended to do.

CHAPTER 14

EL SOMBRERO IN THE SKY

THE MARY TYLER MOORE SHOW was all the rage when I was a little girl. I didn't pay that much attention to it because I was too young to understand it, but more often than not, I was in the den when Mama and Daddy would watch. I vaguely knew the characters' names and had a general sense of how everybody was connected, but mostly I'd just glance at Mary and her friends while I brushed out my dolls' hair, wove pot holders on my little plastic loom, or fired up the Easy-Bake Oven. And really, there was only one part of the show I wanted to see every week: the end of the opening credits when Mary would throw her hat up in the sky.

I didn't have my own hat-in-the-sky moment until about eighteen years later. And naturally I didn't *literally* throw my hat in the air because, as best as I remember, I didn't really own any hats until I turned thirty-five and started to see the sun as my face's sworn enemy. However, I very much had a *figurative* hat-in-the-sky moment not too long after I turned twenty-five.

Perhaps this is a good time for me to tell you about that.

I'd applied for a job at Elliston High School—right outside of Jackson, Mississippi—because I very much wanted to live closer to the friends who knew me best. By then I'd spent almost two years teaching Spanish in Myrtlewood, and I was beyond ready to dig into some literature. So, with my principal Mr. Pearson's blessing, I took a personal day to interview at Elliston, where I was hoping to get a job.

(For some reason it's important to me to tell you that I wore a matching lightweight-sweater outfit to my interview—as in camisole sweater, cardigan sweater, and SWEATER PANTS.)

(That's right. I said SWEATER PANTS.)

(Why'd you hate me, nineties?)

I was scared out of my mind before that interview started—probably because I knew I looked ridiculous in that head-to-toe, coral-colored sweater ensemble—but for the first fifteen minutes, it was mostly an easy-going discussion with the principal, Mr. Dumas. Eventually, though, we started to talk about what I might be teaching if he hired me.

I felt free to chime in with my thoughts.

"You know"—I paused here for a second to establish some really rock-solid eye contact so he'd know how earnest and sincere I was—"I've really tried to analyze what grade I'd like to teach, and it seems to me that ninth or tenth would be better. I mean, I *could* be comfortable with eleventh or twelfth graders, but I really like the reading curriculum for the freshmen and sophomores."

"Yes, ma'am," Mr. Dumas replied.

"Plus," I continued, "since next year will only be my third year in a high school classroom, I'd probably be more *comfortable* with the younger kids—but I have taught the older kids in Myrtlewood, so I guess I'd be okay with them, too. I just like the idea of sort of getting in on the ground level and helping those ninth graders learn how to write an essay, you know?"

"Sure," he said.

Then I leaned forward in my chair and smiled way too big while I waited for him to tell me what grade I was going to be teaching.

Finally he broke the silence. "Well, Sophie, here's the thing."

"Yes, sir?"

I had a feeling that "the thing" and I weren't going to be BFFs anytime soon.

"I just don't think I'm going to have any openings in English this year."

"Sir?"

I knew exactly what he'd said, of course—but I needed him to repeat it one more time so that maybe I could gather my thoughts and form a coherent sentence.

"I just don't think—well, actually I *know*—that I'm not going to have a place for you in English."

By this point I was silently begging myself not to cry. I was supposed to be a professional, I was supposed to be a grown-up, and I was *not* supposed to break down in front of a man who I had known for only a little over a half hour.

"Oh. Okay." I did my best not to look crestfallen—and tried to figure out what to say next. Finally I decided to go with whatever I thought Mama would have said in that moment, because I knew that Mama would have said something kind.

"Well," I began, "I sure do appreciate your meeting with me today, and who knows? Maybe something will work out down the road!"

My words may have *technically* been kind, but they sounded an awful lot like disappointment.

I started to reach for the folder I'd carried into the interview because, well, carrying a folder into an interview is just one of those things we all do, I guess in the event that someone hands us some important papers. Surprisingly, though, Mr. Dumas interrupted my attempt to make a gracious exit.

"Oh, I'm sorry," he said. "I haven't been very clear. We'll have a position for you next year. Just not in English. But I'm almost certain that there's a spot for you."

A wave of unbelief passed over me—because surely not. *Surely not.* SURELY. DANG. NOT.

And then, in the most matter-of-fact way, he said it. "We have an opening for a Spanish I teacher."

And that's pretty much the moment when I wanted to set my hair on fire.

Thankfully, though, I recovered enough to murmur and nod my way through the rest of our conversation. By the time I left Mr. Dumas's office, I'd agreed to accept the Spanish position at Elliston High—pending the superintendent's approval. Sure, I was slightly bummed about teaching Spanish again, but I was elated by the prospect of moving to Jackson, which felt like the first truly independent decision I'd ever made.

I walked slowly out to the parking lot, and before I opened my car door, I stopped to look around and take in what would more than likely be the backdrop for the next phase of my life. I felt like a combination of Melanie Griffith at the end of *Working Girl*, Lily Tomlin at the end of *9 to 5*—and our girl MTM at the end of her opening credits. Granted, all the details of my new job weren't set in stone, but the strong possibility of it felt like a major step forward.

It was my personal hat-in-the-sky moment.

Or sombrero, as it were.

• • •

Every once in a while I wish I'd kept a list of the good decisions and the bad decisions for each year of my life. It's not because I'd like to pat myself on the back for all the good ones and slip into some quality self-loathing over all the bad ones; it's because I think that, for the most part, the things that I thought were such a big deal would make me laugh.

For example, if I had chronicled some of the more trivial bad decisions of, oh, 1990, the list would have looked a little something like this:

1. Letting my hair grow out to one length (it looked like Andre's on *The Real World: New York*, only Andre looked way better with a ponytail than I did)
2. Engaging in a short-lived flirtation with whiskey (some lessons you can only learn the hard way, I reckon)
3. Developing to a strong allegiance to the musical stylings of Paula Abdul
4. Participating in an ill-advised three-day workout kick that left me unable to bend my knees

5. Wearing a blue-velvet dress with shoulder pads so huge that my date to a fancy dance actually introduced me to people by saying, "This is my date, Sophie—and these are her sleeves."

On the contrary, if I'd made a list of my good decisions in, say, 1995, the list would have been short and to the point:

1. Overcoming an obsession with honeydew melon candles that can only be described as a stronghold
2. Finally balancing my checking account, thanks to some loving intervention
3. Moving to Jackson
4. Moving to Jackson
5. Moving to Jackson

Not that moving to Jackson was a big deal or anything.

And it wasn't that Myrtlewood had been bad. The people there were great, and in the grand scheme of my life, I learned more about myself in those two years than any two years since. Jackson, though, meant that I was once again in the same town as my childhood friend Kim, along with my college friends Marion and Tracey. We were all in different phases of life by then—Marion and Tracey were mamas, Kim was married, and I was single—but it didn't matter. It was comforting just to know they lived in the generalish vicinity of my little one-bedroom apartment that was right across the street from the mall.

(I know. I lived right across the street from a mall.)

(It was like all my childhood dreams had come true.)

It was sort of a strange and unexpected development, but from the moment I unpacked my first moving box in Jackson, I was determined to be a more responsible person. The changes didn't happen right away, but gradually I incorporated a pretty good measure of consistency into my life. I stuck to a budget, I exercised, I decorated my apartment, I worked hard at my job, and I finished my teaching certification in English *and* Spanish, because GET A CLUE, EUNICE—THE SPANISH SEEMS TO BE A

PATTERN. For the first time I had a genuine awareness that I was making a life for myself, and I savored it. I really did.

The best part was how quickly I felt a sense of community with the people around me. My coworkers, who included Kimberly, were a social bunch, and from my very first day at Elliston High they welcomed me into the fold. They included me in their weekday lunches, their Thursday night dinners, and their just-because get-togethers. It was a group full of story-tellers, and I'd spend most of every outing listening as if my life depended on it and laughing so hard I might as well have done a thirty-minute ab workout.

I was only about 120 miles from my grad school apartment in Starkville, but I might as well have been a world away.

• • •

In the South there are three cornerstones of society that most people hold in high regard: family, church, and high school football. College football is a big deal too, of course, but those other three things bind communities together. Elliston, Mississippi, was no exception.

At the time, Elliston High School was one of the biggest high schools in Mississippi, and while sports in general were a really big deal, football was the biggest deal of all. The head coach was a man named Ben Johnston, and there was no question that he ruled the athletics roost in Elliston. A lifelong resident of Mississippi, he knew or knew of just about everybody in the state's high school football circles, and when he wasn't at school, he was usually holding court at a Rotary Club luncheon or a booster club meeting. Like many Southern coaches, he was gruff voiced from years of yelling at practice, stiff kneed from decades of running drills, and red faced from too much sun (and too little blood pressure medication).

He also happened to be hilarious.

On Thursday nights during football season, a group of Elliston teach-ers faithfully met for supper and no small degree of storytelling at the Iron Horse Grill in downtown Jackson. I'm not sure when the tradition started, but Kim insisted that I go with her and her husband, Jody, on the Thursday before my first-ever EHS football game. There were enough of us to take up a gigantic booth as well as four or five tables, and what I remember more than anything else was that these people were just endlessly entertained by one another.

On the surface they didn't seem to have much in common other than their Mississippi residency and the place of their employment, but when I dug a little deeper, I found some kindred spirits. No topic was off limits, so on any given night the conversation would run the gamut from peach cobbler to politics to the problems with standardized testing. For the most part, my coworkers were people of deep faith and strong personal conviction, and I loved watching how seamlessly they moved from work life to personal life to work life and back again. There was no separation between the two—no personality that they kept tucked away for one or the other, and the wholeness of their lives was something I very much needed to see.

It was probably the first time in my life when I'd been mindful about looking for it.

I don't know. I guess I was finally at a point when I relished the opportunity to soak up some wisdom, so those sweet people from Elliston High School were one of the Lord's many gifts during my Jackson years.

No matter where we were or what we did, though, our unofficial host and master of ceremonies was Coach Johnston, whose slightly more rebellious personality came alive in a big group. He was loud, charming, and just a little bit salty, and I don't think he ever met a crowd he didn't like. Since Kim and I were almost always the youngest two faculty members at any social gathering, most of Coach Johnston's stories were new to us, so we tended to sit at or near his table while he held court. Listening to him was like being in the front row of a Southern Gothic Festival, what with his tales of toothless fishermen, Mississippi Delta juke joints, and 1960s moonshine runs that always seemed to begin or end on gravel roads that ran alongside cotton fields.

And listen—that was just the first fifteen minutes of any given Thursday night. That was the warm-up. By the time we'd leave the Iron Horse two or three hours later, Kim and I would have heard so many stories that we both could have sworn we'd been in the presence of one of Flannery O'Connor's long-lost sons.

(I am certainly not implying that Flannery O'Connor actually had any long-lost sons.)

(I would be mortified if I started some sort of literary scandal.)

One Thursday night before play-offs—sometime in November, I think—Kim and I were walking to her car after supper at the Iron Horse when we heard Coach Johnston's voice behind us:

"Hey! Y'all hold up! I just got off the phone with Gail."

Gail was Coach Johnston's wife of almost twenty-five years, and I knew from the first time I met her that the Lord had given her extra portions of patience, calm, and understanding. He seems to do that with coaches' wives, especially in the South.

Kim and I stopped just as we were opening our car doors and waited for Coach to catch up to us.

"So, I just got off the phone with Gail, and I was telling her that I won't sleep a wink tonight. I'm just nervous. I need to ride around. Y'all tired? Y'all want to go?"

Kim and I looked at each other, both of us wondering what to do. We didn't exactly have a whole lot going on other than wanting to get home to watch TV, but I think we both wondered if going riding around with Coach Johnston was within the bounds of propriety. I mean, he was very much like an older brother to us, and we felt totally safe with him, but he was married, after all, and so was Kim, and . . .

He must have read our minds, because he looked at Kim, then at me, and then back at Kim, and he started to laugh. "Are y'all worried about Gail? Lord, have mercy. She ain't gonna care! I'm old enough to be y'all's daddy. Now come on, you two—let's go hit the roads of Elliston County."

And then he grinned real big.

Kim and I agreed to go—but not until we got the go-ahead from her husband. The three of us piled into Coach's Jeep, and after he fired up a cigar, rolled down his window, and opened up his sunroof, he weaved through the streets of downtown Jackson until we reached the on-ramp to I-55. Coach turned north, drove five or six miles, then exited on a road that could have taken us all the way to Yazoo City if we'd had a mind to go.

I don't remember what we talked about, what music we listened to, or how long we were in that car. But I will never forget how that stretch of road spoke to me; it wound around and looped and curved in the direction of nowhere in particular, and then all of a sudden it was like the whole world opened up—gorgeous, rolling hills on each side of us, wide-open Mississippi sky up above.

I didn't have the foggiest idea how we'd gotten there.

But I was pretty certain that it was where I belonged.

And I couldn't imagine why I'd ever want to leave.

• • •

My first year in Jackson flew by, and if there's a big, overarching theme to those twelve months, it's this: it was the happiest, most uncomplicated time.

So naturally that's when David came back into the picture.

Stands to reason, right?

And when he came back into the picture, he fully intended to stay there.

Granted, our first attempt at dating was kind of a mess. But the second time around? It was just *easy*. We had a long talk beforehand, and David told me very clearly that, as far as he was concerned, that was it. The intention was not to hang out on weekends and take some road trips and see where everything led. The intention was that, barring something completely unexpected, we would get married.

Well. All righty then. And also: FINE BY ME.

We were both twenty-six—plenty old enough to know that we loved each other and missed each other in the least dramatic way possible. By that point I'd learned that my heart could certainly go on without him (thank you, Celine Dion, for expressing that thought through song), but I also knew that my heart was never more at home than when we were together. Dating seemed like a really good plan.

Six months later he proposed, and my reaction wasn't anything like I thought it would be. I didn't feel faint. I didn't feel like some giddy princess who had finally found her prince. I did, however, feel deeply, profoundly *honored*. That was the sweetest surprise.

And five months after that—a week after I wrapped up my second year in the town that I'd never wanted to leave—we said our vows at the front of the church where we'd laughed pretty much nonstop throughout elementary, junior high, and high school.

We'd come a long way since then.

I wasn't even wearing high-top Reeboks anymore.

• • •

Our wedding reception was at the home of some family friends, and since all the moisture in the entire world had collected over Myrtlewood early that morning and poured from the clouds as if God Himself were dumping buckets of water over central Mississippi, the post-wedding festivities turned out to be more of an indoor affair than an outdoor one. David and I hadn't planned on having a receiving line or anything like that, but it was so crowded inside that we ended up standing in a little parlor so we could talk to people and stay out of the fray a little bit. Within just a few minutes, though, a line started to form, and for the next hour and a half, we hugged what seemed like everyone we'd ever known.

It may have been my favorite part of the whole day. I'm not one to be overly sentimental, but let's face it: people are awesome.

We were getting close to the last person when I saw Coach Johnston at the back of the line. Naturally we'd invited him to the wedding—he'd been a big part of my life in Jackson, and heaven knows he'd kept me entertained for two football seasons' worth of Thursday nights—but it never dawned on me that he would drive over for the ceremony, much less stay for the reception.

It seems to me that every wedding has an emotional tipping point—a particular moment when, for whatever reason, all the big feelings just spill over and pour out. And I am here to tell you that when I caught a glimpse of Coach Ben Johnston as he poked his head around the corner of that little parlor where David and I were standing, that was it for me. I started to cry so hard I wondered if I'd ever stop. I finally had to put my head in my hands and surrender to full-on blubbering mode. David, who was as taken aback by my reaction as I was, wrapped his arm around my shoulders and asked me to tell him what was wrong.

I couldn't say a word, though. I just cried.

When Coach Johnston finally got close enough to hug my neck, I left a trail of mascara all over his jacket (I believe the expression you're looking for is "subdued elegance"). He was, to say the least, surprised by such an emotional greeting, and he patted me sort of awkwardly on the shoulder as he shook David's hand.

"Hey. We're gonna miss this girl," he said. "But I sure am happy for y'all."

I don't think I ever formed a sentence. I did, however, hiccup with a frightening degree of regularity.

And while I'm sometimes confounded by my reactions, I knew *exactly* why the sight of Coach Johnston affected me like it did.

Somewhere in my early twenties I'd fallen into the trap of thinking that if there was ever going to be a long-term rekindling of my faith, the flame would arrive in the most melodramatic way possible. I'd pictured a long walk down the center aisle of a church, probably at the end of a revival when conviction had just worn me down and worn me out over the course of three or four nights. Maybe I'd find myself in the center of a prayer circle, surrounded by loving friends and family members who would urge me to turn from my doubt and trust the Lord more. Or maybe Emma Kate would drag out all those old Scripture index cards from her college bulletin board, and the fresh realization of all the ways I'd most certainly disappointed Jesus would open the floodgates of repentance and sorrow.

Turns out I was wrong.

The issue in the first half of my twenties wasn't that I didn't know the Lord. The issue wasn't that He had forsaken me. The issue was this: I began a relationship with Jesus in an environment where faith was super easy. I didn't have to go deep in my relationship with Him because superficial worked just fine in my safe little life with my safe little family and my safe little church and my safe little friends. But when I went to college, that safe little faith was no match for the big, real world. I had the benefit of good friends to keep any major rebellion at bay, but anything that looked like obedience in my life was mostly just good behavior. It was almost like, when I was eighteen or nineteen, someone pressed a pause button on my faith, and the process of growing in maturity as a believer came to a screeching halt.

But finally, when I was twenty-six, that pause button got pressed again, and I can tell you even now exactly who was responsible (well, in addition to, you know, the Lord): a big ole assortment of folks who lived in and around Jackson, Mississippi—and who had the courage to live real life right in front of me. They weren't accountability partners or mentors or counselors, though certainly all those are valuable. They'd never asked me to sit before them and recount every mistake I'd ever made. They didn't try to implement a five-step discipleship strategy for my personal sanctification.

But they dropped by my apartment with their babies, and they invited me to the Iron Horse, and they stopped by my classroom after school just to see what was going on. I'd met some of them in college, I'd met some of them at work, and I'd even met one of them in the crib (that would be Kim). They were my friends. Plain and simple. And there was something about their unconditional acceptance that met me right in the dead center of my need. I doubt that any of them knew how much they were ministering to me, but they opened up their homes and their arms and their hearts at a time when what I needed more than anything else was to see real life integrated with real faith—in all of its messy wonderfulness.

And oh, did they ever show me. Even when they had no idea.

So when I saw Coach Johnston at my wedding, I didn't cry because I was sad. I cried because I was so stinkin' grateful. Just seeing his face reminded me how those two years in Jackson had been pure grace in my life. *Pure grace*. That didn't mean that I stopped making mistakes—but it did mean I started learning from them. Slowly but surely I started to realize that a return to faith doesn't have to be melodramatic, and it doesn't have to happen overnight. For me, as simple as it sounds, it was just a series of really small turns in the right direction. It was so gradual, in fact, that I'd barely even realized it was happening—until one day I discovered that instead of feeling drawn to the darkness, I much preferred to walk in the Light.

I had a long way to go, of course.

But it felt mighty good to be on the right path again.

CHAPTER 15

BECAUSE WE ALL HAVE FASHION REGRETS FROM OUR TWENTIES

My LITTLE ONE-BEDROOM apartment in Jackson wasn't anything special, but it boasted one feature that brought me a considerable amount of joy during the two years I lived there: a walk-in closet. That walk-in closet was the perfect place to try on clothes or put together new outfits or look back through my personal fashion archives. I kept it impeccably organized, from my casual clothes to my dressy clothes to my purses and scarves and shoes. It was a happy place.

Marriage, however, meant that I'd be moving to Baton Rouge, where David had lived and worked for several years, and that transition forced me to face the Ghosts of My Fashion Past. Since David and I were moving into a small rental house with two very tiny closets, I had to pare down my wardrobe and my accessories, or else we were going to have to turn the second bedroom into a closet. This seemed unwise considering I wanted our house to look more like a pretty home and less like a clothing showroom at the Atlanta Merchandise Mart.

So I cleaned out. I donated. I threw away. And somehow I managed to fit all my clothes in that tiny, two-by-four-foot closet. I can only attribute my organizational achievement to the Lord; He did so many incredible things during our time in Baton Rouge, and I'm fully convinced that getting all my stuff in my closet was the first.

Here are some of the things I had to leave behind.

1. Color-coordinated shoes and accessories

    Back in the day, there was nothing like finding the perfect pair of bright-yellow flats to match that tiny touch of bright yellow in my newest Cambridge Dry Goods skirt. I'm sure I also looked for a bright-yellow bow that I could wear in my hair—just before wondering why I never could convince anyone that my personality was actually very dark and edgy. It was a tough decision, but my assortment of hot-pink, royal-blue, kelly-green, and multicolored flats and pumps didn't make the trip down I-55. Only the neutral shoes had an opportunity to *laissez les bons temps rouler*.

2. Stirrup pants

    Sometimes I wonder why someone who loved me didn't pull me aside when I was wearing my purple or my houndstooth (!!!) or my plaid (!!!) stirrup pants and say, "Listen. Sister. You just can't. I don't even want to go into the specific reasons why, but you just can't. Well, here's one specific reason, and I hope it'll be helpful: those pants make your legs look like fat exclamation points. It's a hard truth, I know, but it's good to know your limitations. Embrace the wide-legged trouser pant. You can thank me later."

3. Bedazzled sweaters

    From time to time I'd "inherit" an outfit from Mama if she didn't love the way it fit or if she felt like I'd get more use out of it than she would. This is how I ended up with an orange-and-turquoise tunic-style sweater that featured pearls, beads, and sequins in the shape of a giant sea horse. I thought it was beautiful and told myself that it made my eyes pop. The reality is that people were so blinded by the sparkly sea horse that they never noticed my eyes. Also, this sweater came with a matching pair of stirrup pants. I looked like a clown at a sea-life festival. No need to take that look to the bayou.

4. Red blazer with shoulder pads, gold buttons, and a crest over the chest pocket

This was one of the first pieces of clothing I owned that I considered to be Very Professional. It went with a long, matching red skirt and a gold sweater, so when I wore all the pieces at one time, I pretty much could have blown a whistle and raised a baton and an entire marching band would have followed my lead. The crest over the chest pocket was a nice touch too; I often thought it would be the perfect jacket for Blair Warner to wear when she returned to Eastland Academy as headmistress. Hypothetically speaking, of course.

5. Cutoff sweatpants worn over running tights

There's no good reason. I don't even think this was a trend. I just decided it looked good and ran with it. Or walked with it. Or aerobicized with it. In retrospect, I can assure you that it was wise to spare my husband the sight of this particular ensemble.

6. Knee-length denim jumper

These were everywhere in 1996. I bought mine at T.J.Maxx and wore it at least once a week with a different T-shirt and one of those little square scarves that we called neckerchiefs. The jumper was basically like a denim sack with straps, and I especially liked to wear mine with clunky, rubber-soled sandals. It was something Brenda and/or Kelly would have worn to the Peach Pit on *Beverly Hills,*

90210, which probably tells you everything you need to know about why it didn't make the move to Baton Rouge.

7. Tiny barrettes

    You know what adds that extra measure of class and sophistication to an outfit when you're getting ready to hit the town (or, in the case of the nineties, just sitting around watching *TRL* on MTV)? Why, try some small, rhinestone barrettes or clips shaped like animals (preferably butterflies or dragonflies, but a frog will do in a pinch), and place them in the front part of your hair, mostly for decorative reasons! I wore these for a solid year. My only defense is that Drew Barrymore also wore them, and she was very sassy.

8. That perfume I wore

    When I was twenty-two, I decided I needed a signature perfume that I could wear for the rest of my life. I picked out one that I thought smelled elegant, but I now know that it smelled like jasmine flowers covered in powder and then left in a hot car for the better part of six days. I'm not going to name the perfume in case you or someone you love wears it (and I'm sure it smells wonderful on you). But it didn't smell great on me, and I must have induced many a migraine, so I'm so sorry, everyone who knew me. You deserved better. And so did David.

9. Two-piece windsuit

    Because there's something special about wearing clothing that your friends can hear long before they see it—am I right?

David would want me to tell you that he had to give up some things too—like his black-laminate, swivel-top TV stand with the smoked black glass—and oh, how he grieved the loss of that five-foot monolith that took up an entire corner of the living room. However, in order for us to create a home together, I had to give up some unfortunate clothing choices, and he had to give up some furniture that was specifically designed to hold electronic devices.

It's no secret that marriage is all about compromise.

And this is especially true when you're dealing with bedazzled sweaters and laminate entertainment centers.

CHAPTER 16

WHEN GOD HIT ME OVER THE HEAD WITH A BIG RED STICK

So. We've reached the portion of the book where we're going to get a little up close and personal. I mean, I don't want to make you uncomfortable or anything, but I'm about to share something that I really believe will take our relationship to the next level.

Ready?

I'm an INFP.

Don't you feel so much closer now?

No?

Okay. I'll explain.

On the Myers-Briggs personality test assessment thingamajig (official name), I'm an INFP. That means I'm introverted (well, actually I'm a borderline introvert/extrovert, but we'll discuss that in just a second), intuitive (no facts for me, thanks—I'll just pick up on whatever's going on by watching you from afar at Starbucks, not that that's creepy), feeling (I'm sure it's a real shocker that I don't approach things logically, huh?), and perceiving (most issues aren't black and white to me; I see all the gray and have to camp out in the middle ground for a long time before I pick a side—if I ever pick a side).

My husband, by the way, is my complete opposite—except that he is also a borderline introvert/extrovert. He is all about what is true and logical and just, so he is basically the only reason I have any boundaries at all in my life. Seriously. He's reliable, consistent, and fair. Thank the Lord. Because I, on the other hand, am pretty much a wet noodle who moonlights as a peacemaker.

People always seem surprised to hear that I'm an introvert, but that's because being a borderline introvert/extrovert is a handy little social tool. I really do love people, and one of my favorite things in life is finding connections, figuring out common ground, and hearing other people's stories. I get terribly excited about the smallest little details (YOU LIKE BRUSSELS SPROUTS? SO DO I!), and I can go to dinner with friends and talk my head off for the better part of three hours.

BUT.

There is never, ever a point during those three hours when I wouldn't rather be listening.

And as soon as I get home from that three-hour dinner, I am going to put on my yoga pants and crawl under the covers and watch Bravo until my eyes bleed. David knows that if he asks me how a night with the girls was, there's a very good chance I'll say, "It was awesome. Big fun. And I can't wait to tell you all about it when I have some words again."

I am grateful that he remains patient despite my annoying idiosyncrasies.

I also try to be patient when he spends forty-five minutes with a customer service representative going over the fine print in an appliance warranty.

Fair is fair, right?

• • •

Long before David and I said "I do," I knew that marriage was going to be an adjustment, so I tried to prepare myself accordingly. Most of my friends had been married for five or six years by that point, so I had the benefit of their stories and advice to keep my expectations in check. Even still, I'm an idealist (please note all that INFP business), so I was a little bit offended that real life set in so quickly after our honeymoon.

Because I'd been in Baton Rouge—known to locals as "Red Stick"—about five minutes when it occurred to me that I didn't know a living soul.

Sure, I knew some of the people at David's work, and they couldn't have been any more welcoming and kind and gracious. But south Louisiana is its own unique animal, full of plainspoken, no-nonsense folks who all seem to have known each other since birth, and I felt like the shy kid who got dropped off at somebody else's family reunion. I was used to being on a first-name basis with clerks at the grocery store, and suddenly I was in a situation where I wasn't sure how to even *pronounce* the names of the grocery-store clerks, because that French influence runs deep, y'all.

I still haven't recovered from the time I saw the name *Melancon* and pronounced it "Melon Cone."

Apparently the central Mississippi influence runs deep too.

David and I were renting a little two-bedroom house in a neighborhood that was "in transition," and what that means is that I would walk down to the K&B drugstore at the end of our street during the daytime, but there was no amount of money that would make me walk down there at night. The K&B always freaked me out a little bit because it was also a liquor store, and there was something odd about running in to buy a bottle of Advil and having to pass by the shelves full of K&B brand whiskey.

(Or maybe my mentality was wrong.)

(Maybe that K&B brand whiskey could've fixed some ailments that Advil couldn't touch.)

The other end of our street ran right up to the entrance of a large hospital, and that provided its own unique brand of entertainment. There was a fairly steady stream of foot traffic in front of our house at pretty much any given point in the day, so the people-watching was excellent, and at least two or three times a week somebody would try to steal a wheelchair from the hospital and speed by our house as they made their getaway. Usually there was an accomplice who ran behind the wheelchair and pushed, and by the time the perpetrators reached the front of our house, fatigue would kick in and they'd start to get winded. I mean, a four-hundred-yard dash is tough enough, but pushing two hundred pounds while running takes a toll—and fast.

Any good strength-and-conditioning coach will tell you that.

And who knows? Maybe people weren't actually *stealing* wheelchairs. Maybe they were just borrowing them to make a quick trip to the K&B for a quart of their famous ice cream.

There's really not a bit of tellin'.

Regardless, during that first week in Baton Rouge, those wheelchair enthusiasts were my primary source of entertainment while David was at work. I didn't have a job yet, so getting the house in order and staring out the front windows were basically the only things on my to-do list. Besides watching *Knots Landing* reruns, of course.

By the weekend I had reached my limit in terms of nesting and ALLEGEDLY stolen wheelchairs. I knew that if I was going to meet people, I needed to find a job—and quickly.

It would have been so much easier if I'd had an inkling of an idea about how to make that happen.

• • •

When I was still in Jackson, I somehow came to the conclusion that I wasn't going to teach when I moved to Baton Rouge. I'm sure this decision was the result of two to five minutes of deep analysis and prayer, and it seemed like moving to a different state was a perfect time to make a break from life as a high school teacher.

And yes, in case you're wondering, I did have another career in mind: *paralegal.*

(I have no idea.)

(Maybe because I kind of enjoy research?)

(And I thought I'd get to type a lot?)

(Or maybe Holly Hunter played one in a movie?)

I was so certain of my future in the legal field that I actually applied for jobs at several law firms. I can't remember exactly what I wrote in my cover letters, but I might as well have said this:

Dear Sir or Madam,

I am writing in regard to the paralegal position that you advertised on April 26. I believe that I am well qualified for this job considering I once took the LSAT when I was undecided about what to do after college. While I'm not at all sure that I scored high enough for admission to an accredited law school, I do know that the two hours that I spent skimming over the questions in the LSAT prep book instilled in me a deep reverence and zeal for the law. Also, I am familiar with a great many cases from the first six seasons of Law & Order, *and I can recite—from memory—the names of the assistant district attorneys who served under both Adam Schiff and Jack McCoy, two (pretend) gentlemen whom I hold in very high regard.*

I also have excellent working knowledge of legal phrases such as vis-à-vis, remand, and sustained. I learned these at an early age while watching L.A. Law, *and* Law & Order *has only served to strengthen that foundation.*

I look forward to hearing from you and hope that you will give me your utmost consideration.

As always, I am,
Soph

I'm astounded that no one ever called me for an interview.

• • •

I'd lived in Baton Rouge exactly one week and one day when I pulled out the classified ads in the Sunday paper and started looking for a job, with my red pen in hand and a notepad by my side. I circled everything for which I might have been even remotely qualified and made a list for Monday morning phone calls.

My first call that Monday morning was to a pharmaceutical company. They asked me to answer five questions as part of a screening process, and apparently I failed miserably, because I never heard from them again.

The second call was to a temp agency. I told them that I liked to type, and they asked me to stop by later that afternoon. Success!

The third call was to a school. Yes, I'd set my sights on a fast-paced career as a paralegal/pharmaceutical sales rep/some-random-job-where-I'd-get-to-type, but I figured I might as well see what was out there in terms of teaching jobs. Plus, it was a Christian school, and since I'd never taught at a school where faith was part of the curriculum, I was kind of intrigued. Much to my surprise, the receptionist asked if I could stop by that afternoon and fill out an application.

Three calls, two afternoon appointments. COLOR ME SURPRISED.

A few hours later I left the house wearing my favorite Laura Ashley dress with my favorite brown sandals. I stopped by the temp place, but within just a few minutes I knew I was out of my league since I didn't have any experience with spreadsheet software. However, I took a quick typing test so they'd have that information on file, and then I drove about two miles down the road to Grandview Christian School.

The school offices were in a building behind the Baptist church where the school met, so I parked my car, grabbed my folder (of course), and walked inside. I introduced myself to the secretary, smiling to myself when I remembered my new last name, and after some quality Southern Woman Small Talk, she handed me an application packet and asked if she could make a copy of my Mississippi teaching certificate.

I filled out everything pretty quickly, and when I walked back to the reception window to hand the secretary the clipboard with all my forms, she asked if I could stay for just a few minutes and talk to the superintendent, a man named Dr. Hughes. What I wanted to tell her was OF COURSE I CAN; I AM TRYING TO MAKE FRIENDS HERE AND ALSO I NEED A JOB, but I went with a more conservative response and said, "Yes, ma'am—I'd be glad to talk to him." She led me back to his office.

Dr. Hughes asked me a few initial questions: what brought me to Baton Rouge, where had I grown up in Mississippi, what was my church background, etc. We couldn't have talked more than ten minutes when he interrupted me and said something I've never forgotten: "Sophie, I don't believe in coincidences. The fact is that we need somebody who can teach Spanish and English. I have some high school Spanish classes that I need to cover along with one seventh grade English. And the fact that you just walked in pretty much off the street—just 'happened' to see our ad and call this morning—and you're certified in both of those subjects? That's no accident. I think you'll be a good fit here, and I'd like to hire you."

I stared at him for what seemed like hours. I didn't have any words.

Oh, but I had thoughts.

First thought: *DID HE SAY "SPANISH"?*

Second thought: *HE SAID "SPANISH."*

Third thought: *BUT HE SAID "ENGLISH," TOO.*

Fourth thought: *!!!!!*

Finally I answered him. "It sounds great to me, but I'll need to talk to my husband," I said. The word *husband* almost seemed like a foreign language.

"Fair enough," he responded. "Just give us a call tomorrow or the next day and let us know."

I walked out of that building with the most surreal sense of peace. I climbed in my car, cranked up the AC, drove to David's office, and pretty much ran to his desk so I could tell him the news.

"Well, I got a job," I announced.

"You're kidding! Where? Doing what?"

"At Grandview Christian—just a couple of miles down the road. Teaching one seventh grade English class—and Spanish." I grinned.

Part of me wanted to cry a little bit when I said it. I mean, it was my *third* Spanish job—but at some point you just have to accept that God is up to something, you know?

"Well, that was quick!" David said. "Congratulations and good for you—it sounds awesome."

His enthusiasm took away some of the español-related sting.

As soon as I got home, I called Dr. Hughes and told him I'd take the job.

As an added bonus, I didn't have to start work for seven more weeks—which meant I'd have all the time in the world for watching more *Knots Landing* reruns as well as ALLEGED stolen wheelchair adventures.

It was a win all the way around.

• • •

Grandview met for its first day of in-service on a humid, stifling day in early August. The faculty and staff were kicking off the school year with a praise-and-worship lunch at a banquet hall in St. Francisville, and while that whole setup was a little strange to me at the time, I now know that folks in south Louisiana will figure out how to turn anything into a special event—even if it's a Christian school convocation where the strongest drink is a cup of dark roast Community Coffee.

As I drove up Highway 61 that morning, I was a bundle of conflicting emotions. On one hand, I was super curious to meet the other teachers and see what the school was all about, but on the other hand, I was totally overwhelmed by the fact that, save Dr. Hughes, I didn't know a soul. That borderline introvert/extrovert was completely at odds, because while I couldn't wait to finally meet some people, it stressed me out that I was going to have to do a lot of talking in order to make that happen.

You can appreciate my dilemma.

After I pulled into the gravel parking lot, I found a spot and carefully walked to the entrance. I've been known to trip and fall at the most inopportune times, and I didn't want my first impression to be as the New Girl Who Twisted Her Ankle before Convocation. Thankfully I made it inside without any injuries, so I grabbed a program, found a seat, and tried to take in my surroundings. There was an array of instruments set up on a platform in front of me, and given my traditional Methodist background, it took several seconds before I realized, *Ohhhhh—those are for our worship time*. I could hear the *clink* and *clank* of silverware behind me as servers set the tables for lunch, and as more and more people filed into the hall, I found myself captivated by the sound of all those south Louisiana accents.

I had never heard anyone pronounce "the Lord" as "the Lard" before. Or mention how they needed to be back in Baton Rouge "for two o'clock." Or wonder aloud if they were going to have time to "make the groceries" before supper.

I was as tickled as I could be.

Gradually people started to take their seats, and I forced my inner introvert out of her comfort zone by introducing myself to a few folks. Several of them commented on my Mississippi accent, an occurrence that was somewhat intriguing to me considering that (1) I thought I sounded perfectly normal, (2) I didn't realize that the Mississippi accent was particularly distinctive, and (3) how could they possibly single out *my* accent when I had just overheard an entire conversation about MAKING THE GROCERIES?

Dr. Hughes opened our service with prayer and asked the praise band to lead us in worship. I'd been to Christian concerts before (HOLLA, Amy Grant), but that day was a first for me in terms of participating in a worship service with a full-fledged band. Everybody seemed to know the contemporary worship songs by heart, so I tried to be inconspicuous as I glanced at the lyrics on the projector screen up front—lest people think they had a heathen in their midst. The first couple of songs weren't even remotely familiar to me, so when we finally landed on "Lord, I Lift Your Name on High," my initial thought was, *THANK YOU, METHODIST CHURCH, FOR TEACHING ME THIS ONE.*

When I was growing up in church, we stood when the choir director told us to stand, and we sat when he or she told us to sit. You were welcome to respond with "Amen" if the preacher said something especially memorable, but the women from the Wesley Circle would probably look at each other across the sanctuary and silently wonder why you felt the need to draw attention to yourself. So for me, the praise-and-worship time at my new school was a whole different deal. Lots of people stood and sang, just like I'd always known to do, but some raised their hands, some bowed their heads and turned their palms upward, and some simply sat in a posture of prayer. It wasn't chaotic, and it wasn't distracting; it was peaceful, and in the most unexpected way, it was comforting.

Well, it was comforting until they started singing a song called "Better Is One Day." I'd never heard it before in my life, and the lyrics were an utter mystery to me. After a few seconds of fumbling around and trying to find my way, I finally just put my head down and tried to pray.

It might not have been a fresh move of the Spirit, but it worked just fine in an awkward-worship-moment pinch.

I told myself that the Lord—and the Lard—most certainly understood.

•   •   •

By the time we finished our lunch early in the afternoon, my nerves had settled and my optimism about the school year was on the upswing. The other teachers seemed super nice, and I was especially relieved to have hit it off with the other two foreign language teachers, who couldn't have been more delightful. As I drove back to Baton Rouge, I wondered how in the world I'd found myself at a back-to-school convocation with a praise band and lifted hands and prayer time that could only be described as "fervent." I'd never been in a work environment that was quite so, um, *charismatic*, and given the faith struggles of my past, I was tempted to think that Dr. Hughes had made a horrible mistake when he hired me. Clearly those people were way holier than I was. Plus, there had even been a moment when my new principal mentioned that we had all been "called" to work there, and instead of nodding my head like everybody else, all I could do was sit there and think, *I HAVE?*

I mean, *calling* sounded pretty hard core, you know? I'd always thought that a call was for people who were planning to spend their lives pastoring a church or living in the mission field, so the idea that I could be called? As a teacher? To a place I'd only known about for a little over two months?

That just blew my mind.

When I got back to the house, I changed my clothes and spent the next two hours trying to will the clock to move faster so that David could get home from work already. We'd been married only a couple of months, but we'd developed a routine of sitting on our tiny back porch in the late afternoons and talking through whatever had happened during the day. Since I hadn't started working and still didn't really know anyone (HAVE I MENTIONED THAT?), it wasn't unusual for my comments to center on how I'd watched *Waiting for Guffman* for the forty-first time—or, on a superexciting day, I might share the details of a phone conversation with Sister or the latest news from the Mississippi State football message boards.

But after convocation day, I had SOME THOUGHTS TO SHARE. In fact, I made an actual, physical list of what I considered the most pertinent details. And by the time David joined me on the porch late that afternoon, I was like a reporter waiting on her cue to go live from the newsroom.

David settled into the chair next to me with a look of genuine interest on his face.

"So," he said. "How was it? Was it a good day? Did you enjoy yourself?"

I cut right to the chase.

"I'll tell you what," I answered, waving my list-o-topics in the air. "Those Baptists don't mess around."

• • •

The rest of in-service week passed without incident, though I quickly picked up on the fact that the tone of our convocation wasn't a one-time deal. The high school faculty met in the library every morning, always with prayer time at the top of our agenda. It had been a long time since I'd been in an environment with such a strong emphasis on prayer, and while I probably would have expected it to make me uncomfortable to know the struggles and hurts and joys of people I'd known for a just few days, the effect was actually the exact opposite. It sounds like a Christian cliché, I know, but it was like we skipped right over the pleasantries and went straight to the heart. For an INFP like me, it was a relational dream come true. I wasn't just learning names; I was hearing stories, and that made a new work environment so much less intimidating.

But speaking of names.

Somewhere around the fourth day of in-service, when the guidance counselor passed out copies of our class rolls, I immediately regretted that I'd never taken French. Many of the last names were ones that I'd heard of all my life, but a solid third were obviously waiting for me to butcher them. I asked a couple of other teachers if someone could help me with the pronunciations, and they both pointed me in the direction of Coach Delahoussaye, a lifelong south Louisianan with an accent that rivaled

Chef Justin Wilson for pure Cajun flavor. Coach D. sat patiently with me while I wrote out each name phonetically (Bourgeois—BOUGE-wah, LeBlanc—luh-BLAHN, etc.), and when the first day of school arrived, I was more nervous about saying everyone's names correctly than I was about having to teach class.

I mean, I think we can all agree that a dyed-in-the-wool Mississippi girl should be spared the humiliation of attempting to pronounce the name *Latiolais* in public. Especially when it has taken said Mississippi girl upwards of four years to count from one to twenty in Spanish without saying, "OHHHH-CHOHOH" for the number eight.

But on the first day of school, I fought my way through those last names just fine—with the exception of an unfortunate run-in with "Hebert."

Listen. I don't care what anybody says. It looks like "HE-bert." My brain took a really long time to transition to "AY-bear."

I wasn't even sad about it, though. I'd totally stuck the landing on Duplessis and DeLaureal.

The new job was off to a beautiful start.

• • •

While Baton Rouge was a tricky adjustment for me in terms of friend-ships, there was almost zero adjustment in terms of my work. Even now it makes me teary eyed when I think about how my students just opened their arms and hearts and treated me like we'd known each other forever. That doesn't mean there weren't bad days because, um, *teenagers*, but by and large I felt so safe and so loved. I never expected it, but school became my happy place. The daily focus on Scripture and worship was transfor-mative in terms of helping me trust and depend on the Lord more than I ever had before.

Honestly, I don't know what I would have done without that place. Because while I was trying hard to hold on to notions of newlywed bliss, the reality was that marriage was proving not so easy for David and me. There were all the normal adjustments, of course—living with someone, sleeping in the bed with someone, realizing that someone really can sing one phrase from a song 152 times in an afternoon and never, ever seem to tire of it—and we weathered those adjustments pretty well for the first six months or so. After our first Christmas, though, something shifted.

I couldn't put my finger on it, but David seemed distant, and I couldn't shake the feeling that our marriage wasn't living up to what those first few years were supposed to be like (my expectations were based on, oh, I don't know—a few British romantic comedies and the first three seasons of *Mad About You*). As soon as he walked in the door every afternoon, I could feel the tension between us.

And since my INFP personality values peace over just about anything and likes to think that there's no relational ill I can't fix, I focused on any and every peripheral issue that might make us better: we found a church, we bought a house, we took some trips, and we hung out with our neighbors, the Boudreauxs (they were such a bright spot, and should you ever have the opportunity to live next door to some Boudreauxs, please know that I cannot recommend it enough). Basically I tried to keep our lives light and happy and carefree and fun (we even got a puppy, for heaven's sake), and I didn't tell anybody that we were having a hard time, because I kept thinking that between the church and the house and the friends and the insert-hypothetical-solution-here, we'd eventually get past all the hard stuff.

It didn't work.

I mean, I'm not trying to go all Lifetime Movie Network on you, but on some level I believed that I'd married a complete stranger. I had a feeling that he felt the same.

That seemed like quite a feat considering that we'd known each other for well over twenty years.

• • •

As puzzling as those days in Baton Rouge were on the home front, I have the sweetest memories from Grandview Christian. By my third year there, I'd transitioned from teaching all Spanish classes and one English class to a schedule of half Spanish and half senior composition, an English elective for twelfth graders who wanted additional writing practice before college.

It had taken me six years—SIX YEARS—to teach some form of high school English, but every bit of it was worth the wait. I really got to know the kids I taught, and I got the biggest kick out of grading their quick writes and essays and journal entries. I'd never been challenged to integrate faith and writing before, and going through that process with my students made me want to write again. Little by little, I started to do just that.

Grandview also proved to be a place of solace and wisdom. I remember one morning in particular when I'd driven to work in tears—worn down and worn out from an argument with David the night before—and right as the bell rang for first period, my friend Helen, who was the Latin teacher, stopped by my room and asked how I was doing. There was something about her tone that unlocked the floodgates, so I stepped out in the hall and gave her the (relatively) short version of life at home. Helen, in her no-nonsense, native Bostonian way, immediately understood that I was concerned about my marriage, not angry with David, and within minutes she honed in on something I'd suspected but never said out loud:

"Sophie. Y'all may need some counseling."

"What makes you say that?" I asked. "I've thought the same thing, but it doesn't make sense. He says that he loves me, I love him, he has a great job, we just bought a house. . . ."

"Sophie. Stop it. None of that matters. Y'all are having trouble. It's normal. You need help. It's not your fault, and it's not his fault—but you can't fix it on your own."

I didn't have any words. I just continued to cry.

"Do you hear me? You can't fix it. The Lord doesn't need you to fix it. Support each other, yes. Love each other, absolutely. Find a good counselor, for sure. But release yourself from the responsibility of figuring out how to fix it. That's not your job."

I nodded my head and tried to wipe the mascara off my cheeks.

"And one more thing," Helen said. "Stop comparing your marriage to everybody else's. You'll wear yourself out, and David will start to resent it if he doesn't already. If God wanted you to have somebody else's marriage, He wouldn't have given you the one you have."

It was, without a doubt, the perfect word at the perfect time.

• • •

Anybody who has walked through an "ick" time in their marriage knows there are no easy answers and no overnight solutions. But my talk with Helen, if nothing else, led to some honest conversations with David about what was really going on. He admitted some particular areas where he was struggling, as did I, and it was so much easier for us to communicate when I wasn't constantly asking what could I do or what had I done or why was he mad. And after almost two years of wondering if our marriage would survive whatever was going on, just knowing that we were both willing to fight was an answer to prayer.

Gradually, thank the Lord, the marital fog started to lift. That didn't mean the problems disappeared, but it did mean we had moments when we could see our way through them. We were all about seizing the day and making the most of the years ahead and many other themes that might be the basis for a Richard Marx ballad.

There's not much about those three years in Baton Rouge that I would call easy. But the Lord's timing was perfect, and He was so gracious to us in the midst of the hurting. He opened the door at Grandview Christian (through Spanish, no less), He led me to a work environment where the Word and worship were paramount, He provided such a sweet sense of community despite the fact that Baton Rouge and I (along with the allegedly stolen wheelchairs) hadn't gotten off to a great start. He gave David and me a sincere willingness—over a period of several years—to do the hard work that it takes to get better.

And don't misunderstand: if the Lord hadn't done any of those things, He would still be just as good, just as loving, just as merciful. But seeing how He had provided far more than we could have ever known we needed was a huge encouragement, almost like an assurance that there was something far better waiting for us if we could just get to the other side.

I assumed our time in the Creole State would go down in our personal history as a season of perfecting a roux, developing an appreciation for turducken, and maybe even learning to hum along with the LSU fight song. But as it turned out, God had bigger things to teach us.

Because here's the thing this INFP learned over the course of several years: sometimes the only way to real peace is through some pretty deep valleys.

It's a lesson David and I were both learning firsthand.

CHAPTER 17

SOMETIMES THE PROMISED LAND HAS REALLY GOOD BARBECUE

DESPITE MY COMPLETE inability to tan or even make friends with the sun, the beach is my favorite place on earth. And since David's brother and sister-in-law have a condo near the Gulf that's about four hours from our house, I'm able to get my beach fix at least two or three times a year. It doesn't matter if it's sunny or cloudy or burning-up hot or freezing cold; as soon as I look out at that big ole stretch of Gulf, my soul exhales.

I was there just a couple of weeks ago, and on the last day of the trip, I woke up way too early, thanks to a puppy that decided that 4:45 in the morning was a fine time to go outside. I tried to fall asleep again once she had taken care of business, but after tossing and turning for a sweet forever, I finally decided to get up and make some coffee and watch the sunrise.

You know, just like I used to do way back in my early twenties.

The water was as smooth as a sheet of glass, more silver than blue, and gradually the darkness started to give way as the sun broke through the early morning haze with streaks of light pink and lavender. Parallel to the beach, a lone boat held course—careful not to disturb a few dolphins swimming in the distance—and fishermen dotted the shoreline, casting and reeling in their lines in perfect quiet.

Perfect, peaceful quiet.

A woman caught my eye as she carefully—almost delicately—made her way down the walkway to the beach. She looked to be in her early sixties, and while it was evident that she was carrying something, I couldn't quite make out what it was.

When she reached the sand, she seemed to have a clear destination in mind, so I followed her line of sight—and that's when I saw him: a sixty-something man, bearded and tan, standing at the edge of the water with what I presumed was a grandbaby in his arms. He turned as the woman got close, and he smiled at her, warm and familiar, as the deep, sugary sand slowed her steps. Once she was close enough, she handed him a mug, kissed his cheek, took the baby from his arms, and sat down in a nearby chair.

The man sipped his coffee as he turned back to the shore.

The woman held the baby and watched her man watch the water.

They stayed in their respective places for twenty minutes at least, and they were the picture of contentment.

They weren't standing side by side, but their togetherness was undeniable.

• • •

When David and I first got married, I easily could have listed the top forty-nine things I wanted in a husband—things like calling me in the middle of the day just to tell me he loved me, frequently surprising me with flowers for no reason at all, and supporting me unconditionally through any struggles that might arise with my hair. Basically, I wanted a husband who would meet all my emotional needs and make me queen of his universe.

But real problems and real life have a way of changing your outlook. In fact, I think David would agree that once all the issues—his and mine—of our first three years of marriage were out on the table and in the light, so to speak, our priorities got really clear really fast. In the past I'd always been fixated on the little stuff: Why didn't he sound happy when I called him at the office? Why was he annoyed when I told him the story about that student? Why didn't he run over to hug me the second he walked in the house?

And that wasn't a one-sided deal. Little stuff bothered David, too. Why did I let all the clean clothes hang out on the guest-room bed? Why couldn't I remember to get my oil changed? Why did I walk off in the middle of a conversation to get a Diet Coke out of the refrigerator?

(In my defense, there are some conversations that require the ice-cold refreshment *and* the caffeine infusion of a Diet Coke.)

(My timing wasn't always the best, though.)

But once we started to think and pray and talk about how to move forward together, we started to realize that dealing with the big stuff—seeing the big picture—is so much more important. And once we honed in on how to manage our expectations over the long term instead of keeping score in the short term? Well, both of us seemed to have a whole lot more grace to share. Little by little we realized that it was more important to protect the covenant we'd made than to insist that the other person jump through a never-ending series of hoops.

And don't misunderstand. I'm not saying that sometimes little things can't turn into big things.

I'm just saying an ongoing crisis in your marriage—whether it's related to family or health or strongholds or expectations or fidelity or whatever—has a way of persuading you to pull the lens back a little bit.

I think that's why the couple I saw on the beach struck such a tender chord in my heart. There was an ease and a warmth between them that was evident even from the balcony where I was standing. And unlike my newlywed days, it wasn't because I thought they'd achieved some perfect state of being married. Because you know what? If they'd been together longer than about four months, they'd no doubt dealt with some hurt and some heartbreak and some hard times. Everybody does.

Do you hear me, single people of America?

EVERYBODY DOES.

But that doesn't mean you just shrug your shoulders and quit.

It means you fight for your marriage. You fight for your person.

And to be clear: I know full well that there are people who dug in and fought for their marriage and fought for their person but things ended anyway—and it wasn't their fault. That breaks my heart. But I'm mostly talking to the twenty-seven-year-old me here: *One day you will see a precious sixty-something couple on the beach, and you're going to remember that being a newlywed didn't solve your problems as much as it exposed them. You're going to know that sometimes God is most merciful when he shows us the depths of our brokenness. And you're going to look at your husband and be so glad that you hoped.*

Oh yes, ma'am.

Because when things are looking mighty grim, you hope.

• • •

It was right before our third Christmas in Baton Rouge when David and I started talking about moving to another city. There was nothing wrong with where we were—in fact, I was crazy about our neighborhood and the area surrounding it, not to mention my school and our church. But none of that changed the fact that I *craved* being closer to our families. Plus, since David's line of work wasn't limited geographically, we had options.

It didn't hurt that we were young and adventurous and maybe just a smidge naive.

We had a couple of other criteria, now that I think about it. We figured it would be nice to be close to a decent-sized airport, and I wanted to be in a state where fried chicken was the go-to dish for special occasions.

South Louisiana was a blast and all, but I was jambalayaed out.

So one coldish January night, we sat in the back bedroom of our house and made a list of places we might want to live. All of them were directly tied to family except two: Birmingham, Alabama, and Destin, Florida. I vetoed Destin because I didn't want to lose the joy of the beach vacation by already living there, and the location didn't really solve any of my oh-my-word-I-miss-my-family issues.

Destin was David's number-one pick, by the way. But when I explained my reasoning, he crossed it off the list. Never let it be said that he has not sacrificed for his bride.

So. We looked at our little list and discussed the pros and cons of each for, I don't know, INFINITY NIGHTS IN A ROW. We also prayed a whole bunch and tried to be sensitive to the Lord's leading.

That sounded very spiritual, didn't it?

That's because I'm leaving out the part about how I worried and fretted and cried that we were never going to figure it out and what if we make the wrong decision and HOW CAN WE KNOW FOR SURE WITHOUT ANY DOUBTS WHATSOEVER THAT THIS IS WHAT WE'RE SUPPOSED TO DOOOOOOO?

Oh, rest assured that when there's a big life decision on the line, I can flat-out bring it with the crazy.

So it's a good thing, I reckon, that the Lord isn't deterred by a little bit of bellyaching when He's leading folks to move to a new place (please see: Israelites) (please see also: *me*). And over the course of a couple of months, He made it crystal clear to us—through some very specific guidance—that Birmingham was where we were supposed to be.

We had no idea why, mind you. We didn't know anybody there, and we'd never spent that much time in the area. But to our utter surprise, everything started to fall into place. With the help of some friends, David got work details squared away. I found a job. We sold our house, packed our stuff, and hugged our neighbors, and on July 1, we bid good-bye to the bayou.

I was so excited that I honked my horn repeatedly on significant stretches of I-59.

Clearly my first objective for our new life in Alabama was to KEEP IT KLASSY, SISTER.

• • •

The April before we loaded the U-Haul in Baton Rouge, David and I made a quick trip to Birmingham so we could look at some different areas where we might want to live. We were operating on total faith since at that point we weren't entirely sure what my job situation was going to be come summertime, but we both had such peace about the move that we felt like it was smart to go ahead and figure out the housing end of things.

I'd found a great Realtor on the Internet and instantly liked her when we talked on the phone, and she met us late one Friday afternoon when we arrived at the hotel where we were staying. We didn't have a huge budget, but since the housing market was booming at the time, we felt like it was smart to take whatever money we made off our Baton Rouge house and invest it in a place to live in Birmingham.

Oh, 2000. You were full of economic promise and brand-new sub-divisions.

We spent most of that afternoon and the next day driving from one part of Birmingham to another. Everything we looked at was either too sixties or too rundown or too smoky or too expensive or too something-about-this-feels-dangerous.

By Saturday night we were reminding each other that the trip had been good and worth it even if we didn't find anywhere to live. We'd gotten more familiar with Birmingham, we'd honed in on a few areas we really liked, and we'd grown very attached to the rolling hills and cooler temperatures. There's a quote by Philip Yancey that says faith is "trusting in advance what will only make sense in reverse," and that perfectly captures how we felt that weekend. We didn't know why, and we didn't know how, but somehow a city that we'd rarely visited and had never lived in had impressed itself on our hearts, and all we knew to do was trust that the Lord was behind it. It was probably the first time in my life I'd been that certain about something I had no logical reason to know.

The next morning we decided to go to breakfast and then drive down a stretch of road that I'd traveled a few times with Chox and Joe when I was younger. Some dear friends of theirs had moved to Birmingham when I was in high school, and sometimes we'd stop by their house when we were on the way to see Sister and Barry for a weekend. The houses in their neighborhood were a little north of our budget, but I remembered it as having lots of pine trees and crape myrtles and mimosas, all of which reminded me of my hometown.

A strong sense of familiarity came over me as we passed by buildings and shopping centers I hadn't seen in more than ten years. I absentmindedly flipped through a new-homes magazine that our Realtor had sent us a couple of weeks before, and when I spotted a subdivision that looked to be off that same road, just a little farther down, I showed the picture to David and said, "We have plenty of time before we leave—wanna go check it out?"

He did, so we kept driving.

I've often wondered if our reaction to that drive would've been the same if the morning hadn't been so picturesque, but the air was cool, the sky was blue, and as the suburbs gradually shifted into wide-open countryside, the scenery took our breath away. We drove up a mountain, back down it, then turned and wove through some of the prettiest rural roads that you ever did see. Dogwood and azalea blooms practically formed a tunnel leading out to the subdivision, and by the time we parked in front of one of the houses we wanted to see, I think both of us knew that we'd found our place.

We'd never even considered the possibility of living out in the country. But I'll be doggone if the country didn't win us over on that drop-dead gorgeous Alabama morning.

A couple of hours later, we drove across town to an open house our Realtor was hosting and told her we wanted to put in a bid on a house in the Far Away Subdivision.

"How in the world did you find a house all the way out there?" she asked.

David grinned at me, then at her, and shrugged his shoulders. "We just kept driving, I reckon."

• • •

Adjusting to life in Birmingham (or in our case, right outside it) was as effortless as anything I've ever done. I still missed Mississippi, mind you. But we were so much closer. And the Lord showed us over and over that He had made a way for us, from our little house in the country to our sweet neighbors (two of whom moved here from Baton Rouge not long after we did) to my job as an English teacher (did you hear me? I said ENGLISH TEACHER) at a wonderful Christian school. And get a load of this: on my first day of summer workshops, I realized that I'd driven countless times by the church that had started the school; it was just off the interstate that I knew by heart from the summer I'd worked with Sister and Paige as I traveled back and forth from Myrtlewood to Atlanta.

Isn't that just something else? I'd traveled the road to the church for twelve years before I ever got there. And that's to say nothing of the Alabama barbecue that the Lord saw fit to bless us with in our new hometown.

But let me tell you something else I realized after that first day of workshops: I had a whole lot of catching up to do in the area of biblical scholarship. And if some of your eyes bugged out when you read that because you were expecting that I was going to make some smart-aleck remark like "capri pants wardrobe" or "contemporary Christian music collection," oh no. I am so serious about the biblical scholarship remark. It was evident right away. My new school placed a strong emphasis on biblical integration in each subject area, so when a teacher talked about, say, what she had planned for her calculus class that year, a casual conversation might morph into a discussion about the consistency and order of God. That was usually the point when I'd think to myself, *Sister, I believe it's time to up your theological game.*

Let me put it this way: I was working in an environment where I'd overhear someone telling a joke with the words *continuationist* and *cessationist* in the punch line—AND PEOPLE WOULD LAUGH. As someone who had never hung out in a lot of Bible studies or learned Hebrew or attended seminary or earned a PhD, I was astounded. So it was no wonder when, one morning when I overheard a lively discussion about dispensationalism in the teachers' lounge, I had two reactions: (1) what in tarnation is dispensationalism? and (2) should I ever find myself in some adult version of Bible Drill, this crew right here will be my RIDE OR DIE.

• • •

There's a verse in Psalms that says, "The unfolding of your words gives light; it imparts understanding to the simple" (119:130). And if there's any one piece of Scripture that sums up those first couple of years of teaching in Birmingham, I would say, YES. THAT. BRING IT, PSALM 119. I was surrounded by so many gifted Bible teachers at my school that I sometimes felt like I was taking in information faster than I could process it, but the great advantage was that I started to see and understand things in Scripture that I'd never noticed before. I'd always thought of the Bible as a series of stories, but I started to see how those stories were connected. The words that had been so mysterious for so long began to unfold before me—a person who most definitely qualified as theologically "simple"—and those words illuminated *everything*.

As you might suspect, this was a bit of a game changer.

In Baton Rouge, David and I had been members of a sweet church that felt very much like the church where we'd grown up (with the exception of a good bit more liturgy and the prevalent use of the phrase, "Lard, hear our prayer"). It was perfect for us at that point in our lives; it was the first church either of us had chosen as adults, and the familiarity of it helped us ease our way into the congregation. We weren't overly involved, but there was a sense of belonging that comforted both of us, I think.

By the time we moved to Birmingham, church had become a non-negotiable for us, so we began looking for one our very first weekend here. However, since our house was so far out in the country, we were constantly confronted with the realization that no matter what church we chose, we were probably going to have significant travel time each way. We spent several months visiting this church and that one, always trying to decide if it was a place where we'd want to drive forty minutes for Family Night Supper. I was frustrated by our inability to settle down, and even when we eventually joined a little church that was about a half hour from the house, I knew deep down that we lived too far away for it to work.

We continued in our state of church limbo for the next eight or nine months, but fortunately I had the benefit of great teaching and worship at school to sustain me. David, however, felt like he was dying on the vine, so when a neighbor asked if we might want to visit a Baptist church that was about fifteen minutes from our house, David practically screamed, "OKAY!" and then asked what time to be there. Joining a Baptist church was nowhere—NOWHERE—on our radar; keep in mind that we both come from sturdy Methodist/Episcopalian stock, and the Baptist church was mostly a mystery to us. I'd loved my Baptist school in Baton Rouge, but it turned out that a significant number of the folks who worked there were nondenominational, Presbyterian, or Catholic, so I wasn't exactly reading *The Baptist Faith and Message* while I hung out in the teachers' lounge.

So one gray, December Sunday, David and I woke up and got dressed and made it to that Baptist church in time for the nine o'clock service. We walked into the sanctuary just as the music started, and while I had grown very accustomed to praise-and-worship music at my two Christian schools, it was a whole new worship day for David Hudson. There was a soloist at the piano with a full choir behind him, and if I could pick only two words to describe the experience, I'd have to go with *loud* and *lively*.

We found some seats in the back (of course), and while I was instantly captivated by the music, David appeared to be mildly horrified. We stood through two more songs, and when the pastor moved to the front of the sanctuary, I knew that there was about to be some preachin'.

Not preaching. That would be a much more formal affair.

What we had in store was some PREACHIN'.

And sweet mercy. Did we ever.

I had often heard older family members talk about pastors who could "preach the stars down," but that was one of the few times I'd seen it live and in person. There was strong biblical content, there was practical application, and there was compelling communication. It would have been impossible not to listen. When the sermon was over, we sang a (lively) modern version of an old hymn, and as we left the sanctuary and walked back to the car, I kept glancing over at David to try to get a read on his reaction.

Once we sat down in the car, David actually spoke up first.

"Well, what did you think?" he asked.

"LOVED IT," I replied.

He didn't say anything for a few seconds, so I broke the silence.

"What did *you* think?" I asked. And then I held my breath.

"Well," he answered as he turned the car onto the main road, "I'll say this: at least they didn't haul out the snakes."

So it was a thumbs-down for him.

• • •

By the end of our second summer in Birmingham, David and I had been married for five years. We still had issues that we were working through, but I'd finally gotten to a place where I could accept that *we always will*. It took me a long time to realize that if there was tension or an argument or maybe even some simmering resentment, that didn't mean that we weren't meant to be together or that we weren't compatible or that OUR MARRIAGE WAS OVER, THE END.

It just meant that we were human. And sinners. And the Lord was using our marriage to sharpen us, to refine us, and oh have mercy, to sanctify us. He was also using our marriage to help us grow in grace, in love, and in trust.

The truth of the matter, I reckon, is that marriage sometimes feels a little bit like a soap opera. You love, you argue, you reconcile, you storm out of the room, you cry, you slam doors, you hurt, you heal, you laugh, and you pray with everything in you that there's no evil twin lurking around the corner.

So what David and I found—as I imagine lots of folks have—was that no matter what happened in our personal soap opera (which, Lord have mercy, we would not broadcast on any network, ever, because I really don't think it would be edifying or encouraging for anyone to see me have a breakdown over the color of my kitchen walls, much less watch us stand in stunned silence when one of us backed a car out of the garage but, unfortunately, forgot to close the driver's-side door), we navigated the twists and turns and cliff-hangers a whole lot better when we were walking the road of faith together. If we were learning and growing together—if we could sit in church on Sunday mornings and Wednesday nights and know that, ultimately, we were about and after The Same Thing—all the distractions and drama of the day-to-day seemed a whole lot less important.

I realize that many couples start their married lives with that belief system firmly in place, but we did not. I'm mighty grateful that the Lord saw fit to lead us there.

And that Baptist church that we visited? Well, much to our surprise, we kept going back. Every once in a while we'd look at each other and say, "We're not really going to join a Baptist church, are we? ARE WE?" But the longer we visited, the more connected we became, and over time it started to feel like our church—not just some place where we were visiting. Finally, after THREE YEARS (yep, you read that correctly), David said that we needed to fish or cut bait in terms of becoming full-fledged members—and his recommendation was that we fish.

So the Hudsons went fishin'.

At a Baptist church, of all places.

. . .

When the Lord led us to Birmingham, we didn't have the foggiest idea why. We just knew that we couldn't get away from it, almost like a physical map was following us around with a big spotlight over north central Alabama. Sometimes it even seemed like that big spotlight was surrounded by strand after strand of blinky Christmas lights.

It didn't make a lick of logical sense.

But the Lord.

And I'm convinced that two churches—the one that founded the school where I worked and the one where we finally became members after three years of hanging out on the back row—are the primary reasons the Lord brought us to this place. When we arrived in Birmingham in two cars with two dogs and all our worldly possessions in the back of a midsize U-Haul, we were battle weary and broken, trying our best to slap Band-Aids on the places that hurt the most.

But those two churches, in countless ways, are the places where the Lord put us back together. Through the teaching we heard and the people we came to know and love, He repaired our foundation, strengthened our frame, and gave us the tools we needed to build our little family.

And as I sit here and think about it, I can see so clearly that He healed us in places where we didn't even know we had wounds.

Between that and, well, the barbecue, we are just all kinds of grateful.

CHAPTER 18

SEVENTEEN HELPFUL TERMS FOR THE FORMERLY WAYWARD AND/OR SEMI-PRODIGAL WHO DECIDES TO GO TO CHURCH AGAIN

DAVID AND I were in our late twenties when we started to make our way back to church.

Wait. I'm sorry. What I should have said is, "David and I were in our late twenties when the Lord began to lead us back to the church," and clearly I will now have to go before the elders to account for my poorly communicated view of God's sovereignty.

That was a joke.

But y'all were scared for just a minute, weren't you?

Anyway, by the time we found and joined a church in Baton Rouge, it had been almost ten years since either of us had been involved in a congregation with any degree of regularity. Then, once we moved to Birmingham, we eventually joined an evangelical church (Baptist, no less), and one of the things we realized pretty quickly was that Christians had come up with a whole new set of vocabulary words during the years when we were mostly absent. We were so happy to have a church home again; we were just surprised that we weren't quite up to grade level as far as our churchy language was concerned.

And yes. Of course. There are lots of things about being involved in a church that are way more important than having a personal glossary of the most important new terms. For instance, knowing Jesus as your personal Savior is sort of a critical piece. No doubt. It's also good to trust your leadership and sit under sound teaching and feel a sense of belonging when you sit in your favorite pew/movie theater–style seat/barstool (in case your church is set up like a coffee shop so no one feels, like, *intimidated*, and also, FREE LATTES). But in our current evangelical culture, it definitely doesn't hurt to be well versed in the lingo.

Plus, you know, it makes you seem holier.

(THAT WAS A JOKE.)

So in case you're new to the latest church verbiage, here are a few key phrases you'll want to know.

• • •

Refining

I'd never really paid attention to this word until we moved to Birmingham, and for a while I wondered if they were partial to it here because of Birmingham's history as a steel town. Turns out it's from the Bible (Malachi 3, I believe—and some other places), and it has to be the church's favorite term for what the Lord does when we go through something difficult. He burns off all the impure, unnecessary stuff and purifies us like silver. This is a really good word to know when you're in the middle of a hard time but want to make sure you don't sound bitter when you're sharing prayer requests with your accountability group. So instead of saying, "I am so ticked that I didn't get the job I wanted," you say, "I didn't get the job! I can only trust that the Lord is refining me!" And then maybe you could sing a hymn or two for good measure.

Season

I am guilty of overusing this one. In fact, it might have a slightly addictive quality. *Season* is the Christian's favorite way to publicly acknowledge that, "Hey, what we're dealing with might be good, or it might be bad, but it won't last forever." Over the years I've heard people refer to sweet seasons, hard seasons, growing seasons, dependent seasons, sanctifying seasons, joyous seasons—you name it. The key to proper usage is that the season must have an element of hardship or joy. That is why I cannot advise you to walk up to your pastor and say, "You know, I just sort of feel like the Lord's calling me to a season of drunkenness. Maybe even a little debauchery." That probably won't end well.

In His grip

As best as I can tell, this has been the preferred letter or e-mail closing for Christians since approximately 1997. When I was a teenager, people just signed off with "In Him," but by the time I started working at a Baptist school in the late nineties, the closings had become much more biblically specific ("In the blood of the Lamb," "In the strong name of Jesus," "In the name of the One Who came to seek and to save," etc.). Over the last few years there's been an emphasis on participle-based closings ("Seeking Him," "Growing in Christ," "Clinging to the cross," "Loving because He first loved me," etc.), but "In His grip" has hung in there and seems to have some real staying power. It's a classic, though I am always tempted to go with a closing that a blog reader suggested several years ago: "Continuing in sin so that grace may abound." Praise His merciful name.

A fresh word

This is another one I'd never heard before we moved to Alabama, and initially I thought maybe Alabama had some grammar issues. But eventually I learned that "a fresh word" is when a pastor or teacher explains a passage of Scripture in a way that's completely new to you. Yes, the pastor has actually used a whole bunch of words, but *word* works as a collective noun in this case, referring to the whole of what was said (I totally just made that up, so I hope it's accurate). You might also hear a convicting word, a prophetic word, a good word, or a challenging word. And technically, I guess, you might hear a boring word or a self-righteous word, but we don't really talk about those.

Give Him some praise

In more charismatic churches, this phrase would more than likely come from the worship leader, and then all the folks in the congregation would clap or raise their hands or maybe even shout. In more orthodox churches, this phrase would probably come from, well, nobody. Because no one would ever dream of saying this. Ever. And you can show your praise and reverence for the Lord by BOWING YOUR HEAD AND SAYING THE ANCIENT PRAYERS AND THEN ZIPPING IT. Thank you.

Transparent (see also: authentic)

This is the modern-day church's antidote for curing Christians' tendency to pretend like everything is perfect. Obviously it's good to be real and genuine and what have you, but everybody knows there's at least one person in every Sunday school class or Bible study who takes "transparent" a step too far. Yes, the church wants and needs to love people right where they are, but I am not too sure there's any real point in the church knowing about someone's painful bunions, their frustrations with very specific aspects of their sex life, or—here's my personal favorite—martyresque confessions. Sometimes it's hard to love someone unconditionally when prayer-request time gets hijacked by something like this:

> Y'all, the other day I just had to go before the Lord
> and say, "OH, ABBA DADDY, I want to honor You in
> everything I do, but I confess, Jehovah Shammah, that
> I am weary after spending the last sixteen days providing
> underprivileged children with an in-depth study of the

book of Leviticus, and even though I am grateful, Jehovah Nissi, that I was single-handedly responsible for leading forty-four of them to professing faith in Christ, I come to You and just ask for a small window of rest, Lord."

Obviously it's good to be transparent, but you know what else is good? Humility. And common sense.

Beth Moore

You won't get a single sarcastic remark out of me as far as this one is concerned. She has had more impact for the Kingdom of God than just about any Bible teacher in modern history, and her faithful obedience has changed the lives of tens of thousands of women—if not more. Her words will ripple for generations. In fact, I think so much of her and her ministry that I'm gonna end this without a single punch line. Willingly.

Stumbling block

When I first heard this term—which comes from the book of Matthew, I think—it reminded me of "speed bump," and I have an annoying tendency to mix them up when I'm talking. So if you ever walk into my church with a big platter of fried chicken when I'm trying to stick to a diet and I say, "Oh my word—that fried chicken is gonna be a speed bump for me today," you'll know what I mean.

Tomlin

Chris Tomlin is a good Texas boy who has written a big chunk of our modern hymns and roughly four million worship songs (this number may be a slight exaggeration, but I don't think it's by much). Worship pastors like to refer to him by his last name only, sort of like they're bros from way back who like to hang out and jam (just acoustic, though) when they're in the same town. Apparently singing the same person's songs over a period of years breeds a good degree of familiarity and also affection. I find this oddly sweet.

The Wesley Brothers

John and Charles Wesley were sort of a big deal back in the 1700s. They were brothers, pastors, and founders of the Methodist church. They also wrote lots of the old hymns that we still sing—the Chris Tomlins of their day, if you will. Or maybe Chris Tomlin is the Charles Wesley of our day. However, I bet no one sang this verse from "Jesus, Lover of My Soul" and then called "Wesley" by his last name.

Thou, O Christ, art all I want, more than all in Thee I find;
Raise the fallen, cheer the faint, heal the sick, and lead the blind.
Just and holy is Thy Name, I am all unrighteousness;
False and full of sin I am; Thou art full of truth and grace.

Stunning, huh? It's worth noting that Charles Wesley wrote "Come, Thou Long-Expected Jesus," which Chris Tomlin recorded on a Christmas album a few years ago, so I bet the two of them will totally be bros in heaven.

Conferences

Christians love a conference. The conference can be about adoption, preaching, missions, women, college students, marriage—WHATEVER. It doesn't matter. Plan a conference about any topic that's related to Christianity, and here's what the Christians will do: SHOW UP. There are so many conferences, in fact, that it can be difficult to keep them straight. Most of them have names that are either action verbs (MOVE '15, ENGAGE '12) or Scripture references (4:13 '17, 3:20 '09). I just made all of those up off the top of my head, but I bet one or two of them actually exist.

(Yep. Just checked. MOVE is a real thing. ENGAGE, surprisingly, is not, so clearly one of you is missing a real opportunity to get a new conference started.)

CCM

You're a Christian now? That's awesome! Also, you can't listen to anything except contemporary Christian music from here on out. It's required. Tomlin told me so.

Christy Nockels

Christian women adore Christy Nockels for two specific reasons: (1) her hair is a wonder, and (2) she sings like an angel. She also sings from an incredibly tender, vulnerable place—and women totally pick up on that. In fact, the first time I heard *A Grateful People*, an album she recorded with her husband under the name Watermark, I cried for approximately four days. I have often thought that if I ever found myself in a room with Amy Grant and Christy Nockels at the same time, I would over-emote to the point that I completely humiliated myself. And it would be so worth it.

Small group

Because Sunday school is, like, *so* 1978.

Infighting

Just my opinion, of course, but this is bound to be the enemy's favorite way of trying to hold the gospel hostage in our churches and denominations. And apparently the enemy's bait in this particular area is dang tasty because we lunge for that stuff again and again. The Twitter and the Facebook make it possible to take infighting to a whole new level (see #Elect #TotalDepravity #GraceAlone #ChristAlone vs. #SocialJustice #RedLetterChristians #JesusWasPoor).

Hedge of protection

The first time I heard somebody pray for this was when we lived in Baton Rouge, and my initial reaction was something along the lines of

"Seriously? We're asking the Lord for some shrubs?" I had no idea it was a phrase from the book of Job. My friend Angie suggests that if you're ever in a group and unsure about what to pray, USE THIS. It applies to every situation, so basically that means it's prayer gold.

Christ follower

I don't know how or why we started using this one instead of "Christian," but I felt like I was just starting to get the hang of "believer" and now we've changed terms AGAIN.

• • •

Once you have a solid grasp of the terms, it's just a matter of time before you'll be creating the churchiest sentences you ever could have imagined! Here are a few examples:

Since I didn't want to be a stumbling block, I asked the Lord to provide a hedge of protection around me.
We watched a Beth Moore DVD in small group the other night, and WOW—that was a fresh word.
This has been a tough season for me as a Christ follower, so I can't wait to give Him some praise at the Christy Nockels concert. I hear Tomlin may be there.

Oh, we are a wacky bunch.

And you know what else? For a long time I think I held the church's idiosyncrasies and inconsistencies against it. It was easier to stand on the outside and talk about how hypocritical everybody was than it was to commit to being a part of it. But the truth is that the church will never be perfect, because it's full of people. It's inevitable that we'll mess up and focus on the wrong things and lump ourselves into groups and thrive, to a certain degree, on our differences.

But Jesus? He is our ever-beautiful Same.

He calls us and loves us and makes us glad.

And even when we have to learn a whole new vocabulary that seems to change every five minutes, we can rest in the peace of knowing that there are few things more comforting than looking around a sanctuary (or worship room or storefront or living room or wherever) and feeling, in the company of sinners and saints, like we are completely and utterly at home.

In His grip,
Soph

CHAPTER 19

WHAT WITH ELISE BEING RECENTLY WIDOWED AND ALL

FOR AS LONG as we've known each other, my college friends and I have loved ourselves a girls' trip. It started when we were at State and would travel to football games on the weekends, and then, once everybody was out in the real world, we'd meet at the beach or get together in Jackson or figure out a way to road-trip to someone's wedding. The destination was rarely the important part; we just wanted to be in the same place and talk and laugh and quote entire scenes from *Raising Arizona*, *Urban Cowboy*, and *Coal Miner's Daughter*. As far as I'm concerned, it's still a combination that makes for a near-perfect weekend.

The dates of all our trips—and there have been aplenty—blur together in my mind, but there's one particular beach trip that stands out. I had been married for only a few months when I met the whole crew down in Destin at Elise's in-laws' condo, and we laughed so hard that weekend that one of us surely must have ruptured something. Everybody was married by then—most had at least one child—and being able to stay up late and sleep until whenever was such a luxury.

Well, I mean, I *myself* didn't have a child, but I have always been happy to participate in staying up late and sleeping until whenever. I daresay it was a real talent when I was in my twenties.

That Saturday afternoon we decided to go for a walk on the beach— I believe we were in search of the rumored location of John Grisham's beach house—and when we didn't find what we were looking for (can you believe that when John Grisham built his beach house, he didn't line the beach with signs that said THIS WAY TO JOHN GRISHAM'S BEACH HOUSE?), we turned around to walk back to the condo. Elise and I were at the back of the pack, way too busy running our mouths to trouble ourselves with trying to keep up with the group's power-walking pace, when all of a sudden the conversation turned serious.

I must have been feeling reflective, because I'd been thinking a lot that weekend about how life can just turn on a dime. I told Elise how it had been on my mind that up to that point, none of us had experienced any real tragedy. It seemed unusual considering the trials other friends were enduring, but in our little group from college, no one was divorced, no one was sick, everyone's children and spouses were healthy.

I said, "You know, it's strange, really, that none of us have had to deal with anything earth shattering."

And Elise, never missing a step, kind of squinted at me and said, "Yeah, that's true. But it's bound to happen. You know it'll happen. Don't you think? Eventually?"

I know exactly where we were when she said it. And I also know that part of me wanted to shake her by the shoulders and say, "HEY! WHY ARE WE BEING SO SERIOUS? WE'RE AT THE BEACH! GOOD TIMES!"

But I was so struck by the truth and the gravity of her words that, well, I didn't say anything at all.

• • •

When you're little and hear grown-ups say things like "Time flies," you don't really understand it. After all, when you're seven and desperate for your eighth birthday to roll around, it takes approximately seventeen years for that birthday to arrive. That's a scientific fact. But after David and I got married—and especially after we moved to Birmingham—I realized that there was some truth to that whole "time flies" cliché. After our little boy, Alex, was born, it seemed like the days became months and the months turned into years faster than ever before, but we were so busy soaking up the joy of life with our little fella that we hardly even noticed. He turned our hearts and our lives upside down in the most wonderful ways, and before we even thought to blink, he was one.

Then two.

Then three.

It wasn't very long after Alex's third birthday when I went to Savannah with some friends, and after I got home and reunited with my people, I did that post-travel bed flop where you're so elated by the prospect of sleeping on your own mattress that you don't even crawl under the covers—you just fall on top of them. I immediately fell into a deep, still sleep, so when the phone started to ring around one in the morning, it took a few seconds for me to process that I needed to roll over and answer it.

I don't think I'd even said, "Hello?" before I heard Tracey's voice.

All she said was, "Sophie," but I knew she was upset.

"What is it? Tracey, what's wrong? Are you okay?"

And then she told me. "Something has happened to Paul."

I jumped out of bed and walked into the living room, trying not to wake up David or the sleeping young'un upstairs.

"What do you mean? Something has happened to Paul? Where's Elise?"

"She's at the hospital. They were at the beach, and he fell off a golf cart when they were headed back to the condo after dinner, and now they've airlifted him to Pensacola." I could tell by the sound of Tracey's voice that she was shaking.

"AIRLIFTED?" Of all the things Tracey had said, that was the word that stood out the most.

"Airlifted. And I don't know much, but it doesn't sound good. You should call her."

"Should we go down there? Should I go to her house? What do we do?"

"Call her," Tracey said. "See what she says. Then call me back, okay?"

Elise answered her phone on the second ring. She wasn't hysterical, but she was clearly in shock. And after she'd covered the most pertinent details—Paul was on a ventilator with the kind of head injury doctors would expect to see from a high-impact car crash, and while the next thirty-six hours were critical, the prognosis was grim—there wasn't a doubt in my mind that I was going to spend the next day driving to Jackson to meet up with the girls and then head to Pensacola.

As soon as Elise and I hung up, I called Tracey so we could start to figure out travel plans.

Our girl needed us. And we wouldn't dream of letting her down.

• • •

For as long as I'd known them as a couple, Elise and Paul had a way of collecting friends no matter where they were. They had both stayed close to folks from high school and college, and after they married, they made friends through church, their neighborhood, their boys' schools, tennis, travel, *whatever*. I can think of at least ten couples that would say Elise and Paul were their very best couple friends—and they were. Somehow they made room for everybody and managed to spend time with lots of different people without making anyone feel excluded. It was part of what made them so special as a couple.

(I can promise you Elise rolled her eyes when she read that.)

(But I don't care.)

(It's true.)

So after I arrived in Jackson, Tracey, Katy, Wendi, and I were trying to get organized for the next leg of the trip to Pensacola (and wishing that Marion weren't with family in another state—because we knew how desperately she wanted to be with us). Another group of friends was cleaning Elise's house, washing her boys' clothes, and getting everything ready for when they came home. There was a different group of friends who were organizing meals and stocking Elise's refrigerator, making sure to fill up the old refrigerator in her garage with carton after carton of her beloved Diet Dr Pepper. Everyone we talked to, it seemed, knew them and loved them and wanted to help, and if I live to be one hundred, I don't know if I'll ever see a community rally around a family the way Elise and Paul's friends rallied around them. It was a sight to behold.

I'd spent most of the drive from Birmingham to Jackson getting updates on Paul's condition, but it was only after I got to Wendi's house that I found out exactly how dire the situation was. In fact, we were just minutes from leaving for Pensacola when we found out that Paul wasn't going to make it. The doctors had told Elise that Paul had actually suffered an aneurysm, which was what caused him to fall, and he had no chance for survival once they took him off the ventilator.

The news was almost inconceivable.

Honestly, there are days even now when I think it can't possibly be.

Since Paul was an organ donor, the folks at the hospital were working to identify and coordinate transplant needs, so it was important to Elise that Paul stay on the ventilator until those details were ironed out. The fact that several people would live as a result of Paul's death was an enormous comfort to her, and she reminded us of that several times when we talked on the phone.

Needless to say, our hearts were mighty heavy as we left Jackson and began our trip down Highway 49.

By the time we got to the hospital that Friday night, it was close to ten o'clock. Elise met us in the parking lot, and while I'd told myself over and over again that I needed to be sure to say something thoughtful and appropriate when I saw her, I totally failed and blurted out something awkward like "Fancy meeting you here" when she walked over to hug our necks. She actually started to laugh, which was a very good thing indeed, especially since it kept the rest of us from crying. We walked into the hospital and took an elevator up to the floor where Elise's and Paul's families had been hanging out for most of the day.

It was surreal to see everybody in that context; we were used to running into one another at football games and weddings and birthday parties, but a matchbox-size, windowless waiting room was new territory for all of us. For about half an hour we sat around and made quiet, idle conversation about kids and work while Elise went over some final arrangements with the hospital staff. As strange as it may sound, we were all genuinely happy to see each other—just not under those circumstances.

Oh, Lord, have mercy. Never under those circumstances.

After she finished talking to the hospital folks, Elise walked back to the waiting room, and she'd barely made it through the door before her mama, Cindy, wrapped her arms around Elise's shoulders and pulled her close. We all stood in silence for several seconds, and then Elise's daddy, Frank, said, "Hey. I've got it. How about we all go into Paul's room and pray?"

Tracey, Wendi, Katy, and I looked at Elise to see if she was okay with the idea. After all, she only had about an hour left with her sweet husband, and we didn't want to take away from a second of it.

"I think that's great," she answered. "And I want y'all to see him. Are y'all okay with seeing him?"

We most certainly were.

Over the course of the almost twenty years I'd known Paul, I'd seen him plow into the guard walls at roller-skating rinks, cannonball into pools, rock his sweet baby boys, imitate some impressive WWF moves, laugh until tears ran down his face, scream nonstop on an epic mud-riding expedition, change diapers, smooch his bride, crank up some classic rock, sing at the top of his lungs, and dance his way out of his jacket and tie at who knows how many wedding receptions.

But I don't think I'd ever seen him perfectly still.

That was the first thing I noticed when we walked in his hospital room.

Elise immediately walked to the end of his bed and kissed his face, just like she'd done countless times before. She stroked his cheek and rubbed his arm and held his hand. If we'd been sitting in their living room, she would have acted the exact same way. And as sad as everything had been up to that point—as tragic as his accident was—the realization that Elise wouldn't be able to hold his hand anymore was the thing that nearly sent me right over the emotional edge. She'd been holding that hand for nineteen years, even when she was so mad at him that she couldn't see straight. Seeing Elise and Paul side by side—well, that's how things were supposed to be. The thought of her having to move forward without him was just strange and sad and wrong.

Gradually we started to talk about some of our favorite memories; we talked about how Paul had cried all the way through their wedding, how he'd fallen to his knees and sobbed when he was overwhelmed by the blessing of his first baby boy, and how he had to be—HAD TO BE—the first one on the dance floor whenever live music was playing. We talked about how he never visited a Chinese buffet without consuming a plate of food, then looking around the table and saying, "DING, DING—ROUND TWO" before he went back for "refills." We talked about his love for Hawaiian shirts and the fact that he had the fashion sense of a color-blind retiree.

We laughed and we cried for about fifteen minutes as family members and friends gathered in the room, and after Elise's daddy asked us to circle up and hold hands, we prayed. It was such a sacred, holy moment that I'm almost reluctant to write about it, so I'll just say this. One of the songs at Elise and Paul's wedding was "Surely the Presence," and while it was absolutely beautiful on their wedding day, it would have been even more appropriate as we stood around Paul's bed.

> *Surely the presence of the Lord is in this place.*
> *I can feel His mighty power and His grace. . . .*

The Holy Spirit met us in a hospital room in Pensacola, Florida, that night.

I don't imagine that any of us will ever forget it.

• • •

I think there's a point when you're watching someone you love go through something so unthinkable and so painful that words just stop. I mean, you can only express how sorry you are so many times before you run the risk of having the Hallmark crown imprinted on your head and then finding yourself stuck in one of those little slots on the greeting-card aisle at Walgreens. At some point you have to talk about something besides the fact that you're sorry and that you'll do whatever you can.

So as much as we cried in the days that followed Paul's death, we laughed just as much—often at the most inappropriate times. In fact, after we finished praying that night in Paul's hospital room, we were still taking in the holiness of the moment, lingering for just a few more precious minutes, when Cindy asked Elise a question in the softest whisper imaginable.

"Essie? Would you like me to take a picture of you and the girls? Of you, Sophie, Katy, Wendi, and Tracey?"

Elise whipped her head around and did her very best to keep her voice down when she answered. "HERE, Mama?"

"Well, sure. I thought you might want a picture! Y'all have always been so close! And this will be their last time to be with you and Paul!" Cindy was doing her best to remain cheerful.

Elise's volume was at full throttle when she spoke up again. "Yes, Mama, we *are* close. And yes, this *is* their last time with Paul and me. But if it's all the same to you, I really would prefer not to have a snapshot taken with my friends at the bedside of my near-dead husband."

Tracey, Katy, Wendi, and I were doing our best not to get tickled, but oh my word, our shoulders were shaking. So when Elise and Cindy started to laugh, the collective dam broke, and we were all so hysterical that we had to bend over and hold our knees.

The next night we were back in Mississippi at Elise and Paul's house. Elise and I were in her bedroom, working on the program for the first memorial service (there was one in the town where they lived, then another in Paul's hometown). Elise was trying to figure out what music would be most appropriate, only she and her sister, Christy, got sidetracked by the memory of how their mama used to sing an operatic rendition of "His Eye Is on the Sparrow" in the church where they grew up. In no time they were both on their feet, clutching an imaginary podium and belting out the lyrics in their very best Cindy-esque contralto.

I sing because I'm happy, I sing because I'm free,
For His eye is on the sparrow, and I know He watches me.

Their impression was hilarious—especially the dramatic delivery of the word *watches*. It occurred to me then, just as it occurs to me now, that sometimes the Lord gives us the perfect words in the most unexpected way.

• • •

The first memorial service was Monday afternoon, and while most of it, quite honestly, was a blur, I will never forget seeing Elise walk down the aisle with her three handsome boys, ages eleven, ten, and six. Paul was such a great daddy, and there'd been more than one occasion when David and I had quoted some of Paul's Words o' Parenting Wisdom with our own little guy. Our favorite was "You will eat the food that your mother has lovingly prepared for you, or you may sit here and watch the rest of us enjoy it. But your mama is not a short-order cook, so there will not be any other culinary options." We also subscribed to Paul's theory of keeping extravagances to a minimum so there was plenty of room in the budget for (1) groceries, and (2) a summertime thermostat set to a cool seventy degrees (Elise and Paul actually kept their thermostat on sixty-eight, which meant their house was my favorite place on earth every August).

After the service, Marion (who had driven back to town the night before), Wendi, Tracey, and I piled in Tracey's car and set out for the Mississippi Delta, the location of the second memorial service. We'd traveled to the Delta together who knows how many times over the previous twenty years; we'd been to weddings, to girls' weekends, to parties, and to Elise and Paul's first house during their early married days.

The fact that we were traveling to a memorial service for Paul felt all kinds of wrong.

We spent most of the trip talking about everything and nothing; it was almost like we needed to fill the silence but had nothing left to say.

When we had first heard about funeral arrangements and realized there was going to be another memorial service in Paul's hometown, I had called a hotel chain, asked about their accommodations in the area, and made a reservation. Being proactive felt oddly comforting for me, and even though it was getting dark when we finally arrived at our destination, the hotel looked decent enough. It was nestled up against the Mississippi River levee, only blocks away from the church and the cemetery we'd be visiting the next morning. It seemed functional, efficient, practical—exactly what we needed.

However.

I think maybe the first indicator that it wasn't quite time for me to pat myself on my travel-planning back was that our "doormen" were a couple of stray cats that were jumping in the garbage can by the front door and—I kid you not—leaping out of the garbage can with chicken bones in their mouths. For a split second I wished Elise were with us, because she would have wanted to investigate to see if those chicken bones came from Church's or Popeyes (Elise has been on a first-name basis with the employees at the Church's in northeast Jackson for upwards of ten years). Marion seemed concerned that the cats weren't being taken care of and thus had been forced to forage for food, but my primary concern was HUNGRY CATS LEAPING IN AND OUT OF THE GARBAGE CAN. That has to be some sort of urban legend omen.

Once we got to our room, we immediately noticed that it wasn't just humid—it was DAMP. Borderline wet. The window unit was pumping out cool air, but seeing as how the humidity in the Delta is about 98 percent at all times, we were pretty much standing in the middle of a cool sauna. Even though the conditions were less than ideal, everybody immediately got ready for bed, which was quite a feat considering none of us wanted our feet to touch the wet carpet. Nonetheless, we were exhausted and went to sleep pretty quickly. Safe and sound, snuggled in our semi-wet beds.

It was every bit as luxurious as it sounds.

We all slept fitfully that night but were up and at 'em early the next morning. And if you've doubted my assertions of the high level of humidity in the room, I offer you one more detail as proof: when I was putting on my makeup, the brush that I used for blush was wet. I hadn't run it under the faucet or anything—it had just been sitting in my makeup bag.

I bet the mold-spore count on that brush was high enough to merit a mention on the Weather Channel.

I mention all of that because focusing on those sorts of trivial details is exactly what we were trying to do that morning—trying as best we could to lighten the mood—but we couldn't escape the heaviness of why we were there. It wasn't lost on us that it had been only fifteen years since we'd put on those blue floral-print bridesmaid dresses and stood at the front of the church while Elise and Paul said their vows. So while our attire wasn't nearly as floral that morning in the hotel, we were once again going to a church for Elise—only for an entirely different reason.

And yes, you do your best to trust the Lord when someone you love is smack-dab in the center of tragedy. But still, it's hard. And it's heartbreaking. And sweet mercy, it hurts.

Tuesday's memorial service was just as tender and poignant as the one the day before. There was a moment, however, when a ringing cell phone interrupted the quiet reflection of the pastor's words, and after Tracey and I very discreetly rolled our eyes at each other because FOR THE LOVE, LET'S PUT THOSE PHONES ON SILENT, FUNERAL ATTENDEES, we simultaneously realized that the ringing sound was closer to us than we thought.

In fact, the ringing sounded like it was right beside Tracey.

Then we looked at each other again, clearly in a contest to see whose eyes could be bigger and rounder as panic started to set in.

Yep. It was Tracey's phone.

Tracey began fumbling through her purse, pulling out anything she could get her hands on. The reality was that only five or ten seconds had passed since that first *RING A DING DING*, but it seemed like a small eternity as I watched Tracey pull lip gloss, gum, a hairbrush, sunglasses, and several ponytail holders out of her purse before she got her hands around that blasted phone.

She finally hit a combination of buttons that convinced the phone to HUSH IT, but by that point it was too late. Tracey and I were so tickled that tears were streaming down our faces, and while I kept biting the inside of my lip to hopefully stop what was shaping up to be an incurable case of the (completely inappropriate) giggles, I was also very aware that if Paul had been sitting with us, he would have been laughing harder than anyone else.

And of course that made me cry all over again.

After the memorial service and burial, Paul's mama's sweet friends, whose history together was almost forty years strong, served lunch to the family and the out-of-town folks. When Elise finally finished making the rounds and speaking to everyone, she sat down in the middle of a table of friends from State, looked straight at Tracey, and said, "So, T, that was totally your phone, wasn't it?"

Tracey grinned sheepishly before she raised her hand—and Elise leaned back in her chair and howled. Hearing her laugh like that was almost like a signal that let us know it was okay to carry on as usual, so for the next hour we reminisced and talked over each other and flat-out guffawed until we were in actual physical pain. We covered, among other topics, Tracey's recent sighting of an ex-boyfriend who did not remember her even a little bit, Marion's junior-year term paper about belts ("There are all sorts of belts. Some belts are made of cloth. Others are made of leather. Belts can even be made of metal. And there are many varieties of buckles, as well."), our profound level of gratitude that we'd gone to college before social media was even a thing, and an episode in the parking lot behind Elise's freshman dorm when my car emitted such a large, black cloud of smoke that I thought for certain we were witnessing the second coming of our Lord and Savior.

Eventually it was time to leave the church—Elise had a couple of appointments in Paul's hometown—and when Elise's daddy looked at us with a little gleam in his eye and told us that if we said another word to Elise it had better be *bye*, I felt tears well up in my eyes.

None of us wanted to leave her, and it wasn't because we thought it would make such a big difference if we stayed. We just wanted to postpone the moment when she walked back into her house and there were only four people who lived there, not five. We wanted to protect her from having to deal with everything that would be waiting for her when she got home, and we wanted to stay close by to help however she needed. But real life—well, it wouldn't let us.

So when I gave Elise one last hug, I pretty much just wanted to crawl into the fetal position and stay there indefinitely. That seemed like a way better plan than leaving.

But then something snapped me out of my I-really-want-to-stay-here funk.

I turned and looked back toward the room where we'd been sitting, and the sight of all those sweet faces from our college days stirred something way deep in my heart. We'd left Starkville as friends who loved one another completely and unconditionally, and we'd continued to do that through good times and bad. The next chapter of Elise's life, while not at all what any of us expected, wouldn't be any different as far as those relationships were concerned. Elise's friends would stand with her and walk with her no matter what. Whatever might be ahead, she had her people. And her people might be going home, but in the ways that matter most, we weren't going anywhere.

Neither was the Lord, for that matter. And He does tend to make a difference, you know.

Elise's daddy probably would have told me that I could have saved myself a whole lot of bellyaching if I'd just reminded myself of that last thing a little sooner.

Better late than never, right?

CHAPTER 20

WHEN I REACH THE PLACE I'M GOING

THE HOUSE WE live in now is a long, rambling ranch home that was built in 1974. Over the years we've learned a little bit about the family that built it: they had three girls, they owned a flooring company, and they loved to entertain. I probably could have figured out that last piece of information even if no one had told us; every single room has two ways in or out, and if I think about the house in its 1974 incarnation, I can't help but picture the lady of the house passing a tray of canapés as she swept from room to room in her Pucci hostess gown. Or maybe the Pucci hostess gown would have been passé by then. Maybe she'd have been wearing some bell-bottoms with a sassy *Maude*-esque duster.

Either ensemble would have been rock solid in my humble estimation.

Our house wasn't technically on the market when David found an old "for sale" listing online, but we were frustrated after a months-long search for what we hoped would be our "forever" home (or our "for as long as the Lord keeps us in Birmingham" home), and he decided to take a chance.

When he called the owners to ask if we could look at it, they agreed. It happened to be in the part of Birmingham where Aunt Chox and Uncle Joe's friends had lived—the neighborhood with all the pine trees and crape myrtles and mimosas.

The neighborhood that reminded me of my hometown.

It was a drizzly, damp October afternoon when we first went to see the house. Wet leaves plastered the driveway, so I held Alex's little three-year-old hand as we shuffled our way to the front stoop. I had already rung the doorbell by the time David caught up with us, and as soon as the owner cracked open the door, I caught a glimpse of the living room.

I knew, almost instantly, that we had found our spot.

Windows ran the entire length of the back of the house, and the canopy of trees in the backyard created the most gorgeous filter for the sunlight that seemed to pour in from every angle. And then, when I saw that the sunken living room had steps on three sides, I turned to David and said, "If we buy this house, I want someone to come play the guitar in the living room. And I want people to sit on those steps and sing. DO YOU THINK AMY GRANT AND VINCE GILL WOULD WANT TO DO A SHOW HERE?"

To his credit, he did not tell me I was crazy. He just grinned at me. And I knew that he could see us there too.

• • •

Our neighborhood was one of the first subdivisions outside the Birmingham city limits, and when a large corporation developed the land back in the early seventies, lots of folks thought the company was crazy to create a development so far out in the boondocks.

I'm laughing as I type that, by the way. Because if you could see the sheer quantity of businesses that border our little suburban oasis, you'd know that we're certainly not in the boondocks anymore.

Back in the seventies, though, our neighborhood was marketed as a place for Birmingham businessmen to retire—and, well, they did. The area also started to attract younger families, and when we moved in some thirty-five years later, that first wave of younger parents was, on average, around seventy or seventy-five years old. That meant we had a lot of older neighbors, which was totally fine by us since David and I are the kind of people who like to eat supper at five thirty, change into pajamas by six, and be settled in front of the TV by seven or seven thirty at the latest.

Seriously. You could move us to a retirement home right this second, and after about four days we'd probably decide the living environment was way too fast paced.

So while the demographics of our subdivision suited us just fine, we weren't sure about how Alex would adapt to a neighborhood that didn't seem to have many kids. Ultimately, though, the house was such a great deal that we decided maybe some scheduled playdates could provide what the neighborhood could not, and we took a chance.

For the first year in the new-to-us house, our neighborhood stayed largely the same. So we went to the park and invited Alex's friends over and in the summertime spent an inordinate amount of time in our kiddie pool. But then, slowly but surely, families with young kids started to move in, and after all the grown-ups got to know each other and the young'uns were old enough to walk from one house to another, our street became host to a big, roaming pack-o-kids in the afternoons. And it still is now, more than five years later.

On any given afternoon I watch Alex and his buddies march up and down the street carrying foam swords and plastic shields before they stage an epic battle in the cul-de-sac. Sometimes the girls want to jump in and fight with the boys, but they're more likely to practice cheers or ride bikes or beg the boys to run through sprinklers with them. When it's cold or rainy, the kids will gather round the glow of an iPad screen or set up a board game, but their absolute favorite inside activity is a VERY LOUD variety of indoor tag that they've christened Elmo vs. Zoe. I don't really understand it and only allow it on days when my nerves are enjoying a significant amount of margin, but oh my goodness, the laughing. A herd of pigs would snort and wheeze less than those kids do.

And while I certainly can't be the spokesperson for Alex's childhood, I think it's pretty safe to say that he has enjoyed the fire out of all our neighborhood fun, because he is growing up in the company of some pretty phenomenal kids. In fact, about a year and a half ago, David, Alex, and I were on the way home after Sunday lunch, and after we turned into our subdivision, we talked for a few minutes about how pretty everything looked: the fresh spring green of the leaves popping against the turquoise sky, the branches of the Bradford pears sagging with the weight of crisp, white blooms, and hot-pink azaleas peppering the rolling hills. The scenery made me fall in love with Birmingham all over again.

We were only a few yards from our street when Alex, who had just turned ten, spoke up.

"Well, here we are," he said. "My favorite street in the entire universe."

"Why's that, buddy?" David asked.

"It's home," Alex said matter-of-factly.

I didn't say anything, but my heart nodded in agreement.

• • •

Our first house in Birmingham had almost no trees. In fact, the only tree that escaped the developer's backhoe was a gangly sycamore that stood (sort of) proudly in the backyard. We planted a few other trees while we were there—some crape myrtles, a couple of peach trees, a Bradford pear (which, by the way, my brother calls "mall trees")—but we didn't live there long enough to really see them take off and grow. We saw them bloom over a couple of springs, but that was it.

At our current house, however, we're surrounded by big, sturdy trees. I'm sure my daddy could tell us the name of every single one, but the names don't really matter to me; I just know that they're pretty and that they put on a show all year long. Every room in our house has a view of leaves, and David and Alex would tell you that I can watch those leaves like they're a TV show. There are even a couple of branches in the backyard that look like they're waving to me when the wind blows.

So when we moved to the place where we live now, I realized that living in a house without a lot of trees had made me forget the rhythm of how things bud and bloom and change and grow. It wasn't the worst thing that had ever happened to me or anything like that—but I did think it was interesting.

Well.

A few years ago we had one of those springs where we were getting pummeled by the pollen, and finally, one Sunday night in late March, our local meteorologist predicted a strong thunderstorm. Normally we dreaded bad weather because one of our dogs hated thunder, but in that particular instance we were excited and hopeful that the rain might offer some relief from the allergy onslaught we'd been experiencing for a couple of weeks.

Sure enough, the thunderstorm arrived at about seven that night. It was loud and dramatic and spectacular—as thunderstorms tend to be—and the rain poured fast and furious for almost two hours.

Right before bed I took our dogs outside for their last trip of the night, and when I walked out the back door, I couldn't believe what I saw. Honestly, I'd forgotten it was even possible.

Late that afternoon our dogwood trees had been covered in buds. But after the rain, they'd burst into full bloom.

Even in the darkness.

And it was the sweetest, most visceral reminder that some of the most beautiful transformations take place during some of the darkest times.

I don't know about you, but I can testify to that.

Hallelujah. And amen.

• • •

In the springtime there are few things I enjoy more than spending a Friday afternoon at a high school baseball game, and this past April, I got to do just that during the state play-offs. My school was playing another local high school, and it was one of those spring days when it was almost like the birds and the trees and the sky and the sun got together and said, "Hey. Let's really show off today. Let's make this afternoon something extra special."

Alex asked one of his best buddies to go with us, and once we got to the game, we could only find a parking space on the side of an incline that would totally qualify as a small mountain, so we practically had to rappel down to the baseball field. As soon as I bought our tickets, the boys saw a friend and made a beeline for concession-stand candy, so I walked over to the visitor bleachers to find a seat. I plopped down next to a friend who's a few years ahead of me in terms of motherhood; she and her husband have five kids—I've taught four of them—and I love and admire their precious family so much. Alex's fourth-grade teacher was just across the aisle from us, and about ten of "my" eleventh graders sat a few rows up from her.

And then the home team threw the first pitch, and we all watched some baseball.

Y'all, it was the most ordinary day. Yes, it was beautiful outside, but in lots of ways it was just another spring day in another Southern city on another high school baseball field. Pitchers pitched, and hitters hit, and as the score climbed higher and higher in our team's favor, we all high-fived and hollered and occasionally even hugged. When Alex and his friends weren't running behind the bleachers, they staged a game of their own on the side of the field.

Meanwhile, in between base hits and pop-ups and home runs, I got to catch up with some folks I hadn't seen in a few months. We talked about life, we talked about the Lord, we talked about the poor guy playing left field for the other team because, bless his heart, it was probably not his favorite afternoon.

After a couple of hours, the game ended. We won by about forty-two runs (this number might be a slight exaggeration), and after we said our good-byes, I called David, who was just finishing up at work, to see if he wanted to meet us for a hamburger. He did indeed. The boys and I hiked back up the small mountain (okay, it's just a really steep hill, but I do not consider myself an explorer) to my car, stopping to visit with Alex's favorite substitute teacher, and after we were buckled into our seats and heading out of the parking lot, I realized there was a big ole lump in the back of my throat. The presence of Alex and his friend was the only thing that kept the ugly cry at bay.

The threat of tears was no mystery. I knew exactly why I was so emotional.

I grew up so immersed in community that I didn't even realize I had it. College was the same. But in my early twenties, I lost that feeling of being deeply connected to other people, and to me at least, it seemed like I didn't fit in anywhere. My Jackson friends helped me rediscover that sense of belonging, and while Baton Rouge (and marriage) required some adjustment, the Lord provided a sweet church, great neighbors, and phenomenal students to pull me through.

But then Birmingham. Oh, Birmingham. Life got so much sweeter after we found you, and part of me is so tempted to think that you might be the very best place of all.

So that baseball game, as silly as it may sound, was such a reminder of how the Lord went before us when He called us here. Really, He's outdone Himself. It's been fourteen years, and our roots are deep. Fourteen years, and our hearts are at home. Fourteen years, and ordinary, simple, everyday life is all the more beautiful because of the people God has placed in our path.

It might sound strange, but for more reasons than I could possibly count, Birmingham has been my very favorite lesson.

• • •

Over the last forty-some-odd years, I've lived in ranch houses and dorm rooms and apartments. I've lived in a sorority house, post-war cottages, and the unfinished back room of a Craftsman bungalow. I've removed all manner of hideous wallpaper, I've experienced the depths of paint-color regret, and I've planted—and subsequently killed—more mums than I can count. I've added stripes to my walls (my late nineties decorative sensibilities might be best dubbed *carnival chic*), I've reupholstered seat cushions, and I've been known to tie a Christmas tree to a nail on the wall if I couldn't get it to stand up just the way I liked it. It's been mighty big fun to decorate and repurpose and personalize.

But when push comes to shove, I'll take substance over style all day long. I'll take deep conversations around my cluttered kitchen table, heartfelt prayers on our tattered living-room sofa, and precious friends who know they're welcome even if they walk in the front door and think the laundry has most certainly revolted and maybe even exploded.

Because while it's taken, you know, *my whole life* to wrap my brain around this idea, what I'm finally figuring out is that when we're really and truly at home—with our faith, our family, our friends, our callings, and ourselves—there's a transformation that has little to do with the style of our house or the numbers on the mailbox. It's a change that turns us outward, that opens our arms, that compels us to extend a hand to people who are standing at a crossroads in their own lives and trying to figure out which way to go.

And speaking of that.

My path to peace hasn't been the most predictable. It's less than two hundred miles from Myrtlewood to Birmingham, but the route the Lord mapped out for me wasn't quite as direct as moving from point A to point B. I left Myrtlewood, moved to Starkville, then to Atlanta, back to Starkville, then to Myrtlewood, to Jackson, and finally to Baton Rouge before I ever made it to Birmingham. That route is more than 1,400 miles, which means that, from a purely human perspective, it's about 1,200 miles away from making good sense. If I'd sat down with a road atlas and a pen when I was seventeen years old and getting ready to leave for college, I would have never picked such an out-of-the-way, seemingly nonsensical path.

But God knew better. He knows better. He's been so sweet to lead me exactly where I needed to be—and in every single place, I've seen more of His goodness, more of His love, and more of His character. He has shown me all those things through His Word, certainly, and through the people I've met at different points along the road.

So while David and I really do believe that God wants us in Birmingham right now—and while it really does feel like this is our place—I'm also mindful that it might not be our last stop. And that's okay. I only have to look back over the course of my life to know that if the Lord has another destination in mind for our little family, we can trust Him. He won't lead us somewhere new and then abandon us; after all, just look at what Moses said to Joshua: "It is the LORD who goes before you. He will be with you; he will not leave you or forsake you. Do not fear or be dismayed" (Deuteronomy 31:8).

Maybe things would have gone more smoothly for Moses and the Israelites if they'd had access to the Google. Maybe they would have made it to Canaan in record time if they'd only had an app to help them navigate the wilderness. But they actually had something even better, and so do we:

a sovereign, steady Compass. The Lord guides us along every step of our journey.

His timing is perfect.

He doesn't waste a bit of our wandering.

And His faithfulness teaches a truth we can take with us no matter where we go:

'Tis Grace that brought me safe thus far
And Grace will lead me home.

ACKNOWLEDGMENTS

To BILL JENSEN: You are calm, wise, and honest, so basically you're the perfect agent. Thank you for your constant encouragement and sage advice.

To Stephanie Rische: I still haven't figured out how you crawl in my head when you edit, but I've decided that you must be secretly Southern. I am so grateful for you. Thanks for taking my words and making them better.

To Carol Traver: Somehow you manage to take the most stressful process I have ever experienced and make it feel like a relaxing board game. By a fire. With exotic coffees. Thanks for being patient and taking care of all the details that totally stress me out. You are a gem.

To the Tyndale marketing and sales teams: Thanks to y'all, people can actually find my books in places other than the trunk of my car. I am forever indebted to you for your creativity and hard work.

To Lisa Jackson: There are few things that make me happier than a long e-mail from you. Your insight is invaluable, as is your feedback. You've taught me so much, and I can never thank you enough.

To the sweetest blog readers in all the land: Hey, remember when I quit blogging for about three months so I could finish this book? Y'all were so sweet about that. Your e-mails and tweets and comments and prayers kept me going, and even as I type this, I'm super happy that we now have tons of time to discuss TV and bacon and mascara again. Y'all are the best.

To my writer friends: Thanks for being a safe place to vent/cry/celebrate/doubt/discuss Bravo/analyze cover options/laugh/quit/start over again. Y'all are a gift.

To Jean: You are such a blessing to our family (and to so many other people too). The Hudsons are crazy about you.

To the Baptist and Anglican Council of Mamas: Now it is time for queso.

To Mary Jo, Anne, and Leslie: I can never repay you for all your prayers, but I do hope I get to fry you some chicken real soon.

To Ree: Who is kinder, more generous, and more encouraging than you are? Nobody, that's who.

To my forever friends: I don't even know what to say except that y'all are the best friends a girl could ever want. Thanks for letting me share some of our stories.

To Paul IV, Gillian, and Graham: I'm so happy to be able to introduce your daddy to the people who read this book. He would be so incredibly proud of each one of you.

To Melanie: Oh, my friend. I would have never finished this book without you, especially when I hit that point when I no longer had PLENTY OF TIME. I think our good friend the apostle Paul says it best: "I have never stopped thanking God for you." I will forever contend that you're the best gift the Internet ever gave me.

To Rose: You are the world's best writing cheerleader. Thanks for praying, for checking on my progress, and for sharing 13-B more times than I can count. You take care of your people so selflessly and so well.

To Mama, Daddy, Martha, and the rest of my family: You have been patient and supportive all my life, but never more than this last year. And now that this book is finished, we are going to take A LOT of trips. I love y'all.

To Alex: You're my favorite person in the whole world. Being your mama is the best part of every single day. Your daddy and I are so proud of you. Go get 'em, #44.

To David: You have championed all this writing stuff without condition or hesitation, and you will never know what a gift that has been to me. You read every word of this book before anyone else, and I have to say that you've become a mighty fine editor, Mr. Hudson. There's no earthly opinion I value more. I love you.

And finally, to Jesus: "Here I raise my Ebenezer;/Hither by Thy help I'm come;/And I hope, by Thy good pleasure,/Safely to arrive at home."

ABOUT THE AUTHOR

WITH AN URGE to document the hilarity of family life, Sophie Hudson began writing her blog in 2005. She's just as shocked as she can be that people are still reading. Sophie hopes that through her stories, women find encouragement and hope in the everyday, joy-filled moments of life. In addition to her blog, BooMama.net, Sophie is the author of *A Little Salty to Cut the Sweet* and also serves as co-emcee for LifeWay's annual dotMOM event. Sophie is a wife, mama, daughter, sister, and friend. She adores her family and loves to laugh. She also loves the DVR, Mississippi State sports, unsweetened ice tea, pedicures, and Jesus, whom she loves most of all. Sophie makes her home in Birmingham, Alabama.

Connect with her in the following places:

Blog: BooMama.net

Facebook:www.facebook.com/SophieHudsonBooMama

Twitter: @boomama

For more from Sophie...

CHAPTER ONE

Not to Mention That Her Apple Tarts Would Change Your Whole Life

So, I HAVE A THEORY.

It's not a theory about science or religion or politics. Oh, heavens, no. That would be a complete departure from the very fiber of my personality.

But I do have a theory about memory. More specifically, I have a theory about how we remember people.

Are you ready?

Prepare to be underwhelmed, my friends.

My theory is that we typically have one dominant "fallback" memory that becomes our go-to mental image when we think about somebody.

Now that I've typed that out, by the way, I'm thinking that maybe it's not so much a *theory* as a loose, unverifiable observation.

But let's just run with it. Because whenever I think about Papaw Sims, for example, I picture him leaning over his deep freeze and asking if I'd rather have chocolate, vanilla, or straw-berry ice cream. Whenever I think about Uncle Joe, I picture him dozing in his recliner with a stack of paperwork on his lap—and a ten-key adding machine within arm's reach. And whenever I think about Mamaw Davis, my maternal grandmother, I picture her looking over her shoulder and grinning while she's standing at the stove. Maybe even scooping a little Crisco out of the can.

The mental picture of Mamaw standing at the stove is one of the most enduring images of my childhood, mainly because she stood at that stove so faithfully. She cooked three hot meals a day, seven days a week. There was never anything made from a box, either—no powdery macaroni and cheese or Hamburger Helper. Oh, no, ma'am. There was hot cornbread, beef stroganoff over rice, pot roast with carrots and potatoes, fried chicken, creamed potatoes, fresh peas, fried squash, fried okra (I have to pause for a moment whenever I mention Mamaw's fried okra and give it the reverence and honor that it is due), egg custard pie, pound cake—I could go on and on.

We didn't have all that food at one time, mind you, or else we'd have alternated trips to Mamaw's table with trips to the cardiac care unit, but there was always something delicious and homemade on that stove. Mamaw didn't think she was doing anything special—she was just taking care of her family the best way she knew how—but I think her children and grandchildren can all testify to the fact that those meals she cooked ministered to us like a good Sunday sermon. And she didn't have to say a single word.

For at least one week a summer—sometimes more—my mama and my daddy, along with my aunt Choxie, who is Mama's sister, and Chox's husband, my uncle Joe, would ship my cousin Paige and me off to Mamaw and Papaw Davis's pretty white farmhouse in Moss Rose, Mississippi—about thirty minutes from my hometown of Myrtlewood. Since Paige would have been born in the early 1900s if she'd had any say in the matter, she thrived on Mamaw and Papaw's farm. She was perfectly content to pick blackberries, walk through the chicken coops, amble about in the pastures, and count cows. I, on the other hand, was a total scaredy-cat, wary of tall grass that made me itch and bumblebees that refused to be swatted away.

I had issues when I was indoors, too. When Paige and I would go to bed at night, exhausted from our day's adventures, I'd usually make it ten or fifteen minutes before I'd sprint down the hall and crawl into bed with Mamaw and Papaw. Every floorboard creak sounded to me like imminent danger, so I settled into sleep much more easily underneath the cool hum of the AC window unit in my grandparents' room. No way could the boogeyman get me in there. Not on Papaw's watch. He was broad shouldered, barrel chested, and utterly devoted to his family—a security blanket in human form.

Papaw had some health problems when I was ten, and not too long afterward he and Mamaw decided to downsize and find a smaller house with a lot less land. Somebody later told my mama that Papaw was thinking ahead—he was worried something would happen to him and Mamaw would be stuck with the responsibilities of the farm. On top of that, he didn't want her to be living in a relatively remote area all by herself. So they sold the farmhouse (and the farm) and moved to a blond brick house that was just catty-corner from Moss Rose's Methodist church.

Papaw added a den to the back of the new-to-them house so there would be a nice big gathering place for the family, and when we had our first Sunday lunch there a month or so after they moved in, Mamaw stood at her new stove and carried out the ministry of the homemade chicken pie just like she'd always done. Paige and I missed the backyard of the old house and the pipe swing with the eight-foot chain that hung from the branches of an old oak tree, but there was a barn to explore and plenty of room to roam. That was all we needed.

The following winter Mama and Chox hosted a tea at Mamaw and Papaw's house to celebrate their fiftieth wedding anniversary. Mama and Choxie's brother, Bill, who lived three hours away, was there too, and in my opinion Bill's presence always elevated a family gathering a couple of notches. He drove a sports car, reminded me of Burt Reynolds, and delivered one-liners better than anybody else I knew. If that weren't enough, Mama and Chox let Paige and me serve the punch, and we were certain such a grown-up responsibility meant we'd hit the big time. Papaw wore his nicest suit, and Mamaw wore a pretty dress that she'd made for the occasion, along with a corsage that Sister had bought for her at a florist's shop in Myrtlewood. They made an adorable couple.

Papaw's personality came alive in a big group of folks, so he was in his element that afternoon. Mamaw, on the other hand, was much more introverted and soft spoken. Every once in a while Papaw would put his hand on her back and whisper, "You doing okay, Lucy?"

She'd grin and say, "I'm fine, John."

But even at eleven years old I knew it was hard for her to be the center of attention. Her sweet, servant spirit shone just fine without the aid of any limelight, and part of me wondered if she wasn't going to sneak out of her own anniversary party so she could get in the kitchen and make everybody some chicken and dumplings. She hung in there with the socializing, though, and she stood by Papaw's side until the front door closed and Mama and Chox practically raced to see who could be the first one to take off her high-heeled shoes.

What none of us knew at the time, though, was how much Mamaw was struggling with her health. Then again, not even *she* knew how sick she was. Having been plagued by a general feeling of weakness as well as liver problems during the past several years, she initially thought that she was dealing with more of the same. Over the next few months, however, she and Papaw traveled to Myrtlewood almost weekly for doctor's visits, and early that fall—about eight months after their fiftieth anniversary—Papaw told the family that the doctor had confirmed their worst fear: cancer. Other than helping Mamaw manage her pain and keeping her as comfortable as possible, there wasn't much the doctors could do.

Mamaw was admitted to the hospital in Myrtlewood right before Thanksgiving, and for the next two weeks Mama, Chox, and Papaw rarely left her side. Mama would pick up Paige and me from school—we were fourteen and twelve at that point—and we'd do our homework in the waiting room down the hall from Mamaw's room while we drank Cokes and ate Dolly Madison fruit pies from the vending machine. Mama or Chox would take us downstairs to the hospital cafeteria for supper, and we'd eventually go home whenever they felt Mamaw was settled for the night. It broke their hearts to see her in pain, and they took their role as her advocates very seriously. It wasn't quite like Shirley MacLaine at the nurses' station in *Terms of Endearment*—Mama and Chox were far too polite to make a scene—but in their own Southern ways, they didn't mess around.

By mid-December the weather had turned windy and cold, and Mamaw showed no signs of getting better. One Tuesday night Papaw needed to drive back to Moss Rose to get a change of clothes and a few other things, and since Mama and Chox didn't want him to stay at the house by himself, they suggested that he take Paige and me with him. We had school the next day, but they were far more worried about Papaw than about our missing an hour of social studies. So off we went.

The ride to Moss Rose in Papaw's Oldsmobile 88 was a quiet one, and by the time we arrived at Mamaw and Papaw's house, we were all pretty worn out. It was the first time I'd walked through their back door without immediately seeing Mamaw standing at the stove, and while we didn't stop and take time to vocalize our feelings or anything like that, I think it's safe to say that we all felt her absence.

Paige and I brushed our teeth in silence that night, standing in the guest bath that always smelled like a combination of rubbing alcohol and Mercurochrome. We walked down the hall to tell Papaw good-night and found him lying on top of the bedspread, staring at the ceiling with his arms crossed over his chest. Paige and I sat down beside him, not really knowing what to say. Papaw spoke up first and uttered six words that have stayed with me for more than thirty years.

"She was mighty sweet, wasn't she?"

It struck me as strange that he used the past tense, but Paige and I certainly didn't correct him. We tried our best to comfort him as his shoulders began to shake and the tears started to fall. And while I don't have any idea what time it was when Paige and I finally fell asleep, I do know that Papaw's quiet sobs were the last sound either of us heard.

Early the next morning, around five o'clock, there was a knock on the door. Mama, Daddy, Chox, and Joe had come to tell us what Papaw's heart had told him the night before.

Up to that point in my life—and I was every bit of twelve

years old—I'd been all about ballet lessons, my snazzy new Merlin game, *American Top 40*, and Nancy Drew mysteries. So for me, Mamaw's death was my first glimpse into what family life looks like in the midst of sadness and grief and heartache. I couldn't have put words to it at the time, I don't think, but somehow I could sense that there was beauty in all that brokenness, that there were little patches of light that permeated the darkness. Yes, there was sorrow and pain—but there was also love and comfort and laughter and joy. There was a confidence that something bigger was at work, an assurance of "an eternal glory that far outweighs them all" (2 Corinthians 4:17, NIV).

So while Mamaw's death certainly isn't my happiest memory, I can honestly say that it will forever be one that I treasure. Because that memory, by God's grace, continues to teach me.

And even now, more than three decades later, I hold that memory in my heart real tight.

And I watch.

And I listen.

Try these other titles from Tyndale House Publishers: